The LIFE of CHAITANYA MAHAPRABHU

A Brief History of the 15th-Century Spiritual Revolutionary

Swami B. B. Bodhayan

MANDALA

San Rafael Los Angeles London

Contents

The LIFE of CHAITANYA MAHAPRABHU

Author's Note

Śrīmad Bhagavad-gītā is the direct dialogue between the Supreme Lord Śrī Kṛṣṇa and Arjuna. The reason for Kṛṣṇa's appearance, from time to time in this material world, is to save saintly persons and destroy the demoniac personalities:

paritrāṇāya sādhūnāṁ
vināśāya ca dṣkṛtām
dharma-saṁstāpanārthāya
sambhavāmi yuge

(*Bhagavad-gītā* 4.8)

The Supreme Lord is eternal, but to fulfill the desire of the devotees in the parental mellow (*vātsalya* rasa), He manifested the pastime of being born. When the entire society was in turbulence—the *brāhmaṇa* caste was hating other castes, the king was torturing the civilians, and so on—the Supreme Lord Kṛṣṇa appeared in the form of Lord Chaitanya to maintain equilibrium between various relations, keep balance in society, and to deliver all from this miserable condition.

There are many abridged biographies of Lord Chaitanya available. However, my goal in writing this book is to inform the general audience that Śrī Kṛṣṇa appeared in the form of Lord Chaitanya to deliver all fallen souls by distributing His love without discrimination. To help us realize the taste of divine love, He taught us how to surrender by His own example. We know from Śrīla Bhaktivinoda Ṭhākura that surrender is the soul of devotional practice:

atyanta durlabha prema koribāre dāna
śikhāya śaraṇāgati bhakatera prāṇa
(Śrī *Kṛṣṇa-Caitanya Prabhu Jīve Dayā Kori*, Verse 2)

Many scriptures state that Lord Chaitanya is non-different from Lord Kṛṣṇa. Although Lord Chaitanya is Kṛṣṇa Himself, He took the role of being His own devotee to deliver the people of the world. To spread the chanting of the holy name of the Supreme Lord, which will ultimately give us the taste of divine love, Lord Chaitanya took the renounced order (*sannyāsa*). As a *sannyāsī*, He was known as Śrī Kṛṣṇa Chaitanya.

Once, Śrī Kṛṣṇa Chaitanya said,

pṛthivīte āche yata nagarādi grāma
sarvatra pracāra haibe mora nāma
(*Caitanya-bhāgavata, Antya-khaṇḍa* 4.126)

"My name will be spread in as many villages and towns as there are in this world."

He also said, "The entire world is like a garden, and I am only one gardener. How can I pick up all the fruits and distribute them to everyone?" He thus ordered everyone to help distribute this love.

ekalā mālākāra āmi kāhāṅ kāhāṅ yāba
ekalā vā kata phala pāḍiyā vilāba

ekalā uṭhāñā dite haya pariśrama
keha pāya, keha nā pāya, rahe mane bhrama

ataeva āmi ājñā diluṅ sabākāre
yāhāṅ tāhāṅ prema-phala deha' yāre tāre
(*Caitanya-caritāmṛta, Ādi-līlā*, 9.34-36)

Once, while Śrī Kṛṣṇa Chaitanya was in South India to spread the message of the holy name, He went to a place known as Kūrma Kṣetra, where He was hosted by a *brāhmaṇa*. After a few days of associating with Lord Chaitanya, the *brāhmaṇa* wanted to go along with Mahāprabhu. At that time, Mahāprabhu told him:

prabhu kahe, — "aiche bāt kabhu nā kahibā
gṛhe rahi' kṛṣṇa-nāma nirantara laibā

yāre dekha, tāre kaha 'kṛṣṇa'-upadeśa
āmāra ājnāya guru hanā tāra' ei deśa

kabhu nā bādhibe tomāra viṣaya-taraṅga
punarapi ei ṭhāñi pābe mora saṅga"
(*Caitanya-caritāmṛta, Madhya-līlā* 7.127-129)

"Never say such words. Stay at home and constantly chant the names of Kṛṣṇa. Whoever you see, tell them about Kṛṣṇa. On My order, become a *śikṣā-guru* and deliver the world. The waves of material attachment will never bind you; you will get My association again in this place."

He gave everyone the order to spread His names: *Hare Kṛṣṇa Hare Kṛṣṇa Kṛṣṇa Kṛṣṇa Hare Hare Hare Rama Hare Rama Rama Rama Hare Hare*. Lord Chaitanya said to Haridāsa Ṭhākura:

āpane ācare keha, nā kare pracāra
pracāra karena keha, nā karena ācara

'ācāra' 'prācara', —nāmera karaha 'dui' kārya,
tumi—sarva-guru. tumi jagatera ārya
(*Caitanya-caritāmṛta, Antya-līlā* 4.102-103)

"Some people practice the devotional principles but do not preach, while others preach without practicing. Engage in both practicing and preaching; in this way, you will be considered the instructing spiritual master (*śikṣā-guru*) of everyone, and you will be considered the world's most honorable personality."

We have seen Lord Chaitanya Himself preach and inspire people to chant the Hare Kṛṣṇa *mahā-mantra*, but personally, He did not give initiation. He also did not establish any temples. He taught us to spread *saṅkīrtana* without having any ulterior motives. Our spiritual lineage consisting of His Divine Grace Saccidānanda Bhaktivinoda Ṭhākura; His Divine Grace

Śrīla Prabhupāda, Bhaktisiddhānta Sarasvatī Ṭhākura; my spiritual master, His Divine Grace Śrīla Bhakti Pramode Purī Gosvāmī Ṭhākura; and other Gauḍīya *ācāryas* all follow in the footsteps of Lord Chaitanya. If anyone follows the principle of "first preserve then propagate," then one shall be delivered from this material world.

I hope the readers will excuse any mistakes that may be present in the book and relish the nectarean pastimes of Lord Chaitanya.

Introduction

Two prominent biographies of Śrī Chaitanya have been written: *Śrī Caitanya-bhāgavata,* by Vṛndāvana dāsa Ṭhākura in sixteenth-century Bengal, and *Śrī Chaitanya-caritāmṛta,* by Śrīla Kṛṣṇadāsa Kavirāja Gosvāmī in seventeenth-century Vrindavan. It is upon the foundation of these historical accounts that this book, *The Life of Chaitanya Mahaprabhu,* has been authored. Swami B. B. Bodhayan felt the best introduction for this literary work would be to include words from his previous teachers. The following sections are translated summaries and excerpts from the introductions of Bengali publications of *Śrī Caitanya-bhāgavata* and *Śrī Caitanya-caritāmṛta* by Śrīla Bhakti Pramode Purī Gosvāmī Ṭhākura and Śrīla Bhaktisiddhānta Sarasvatī Ṭhākura Prabhupāda.

Summary Translation of the Introduction to *Śrī Caitanya-bhāgavata*

by Śrīla Bhakti Pramode Purī Gosvāmī Ṭhākura

[Śrīla Bhakti Pramode Purī Gosvāmī Ṭhākura wrote the following in the introduction of the Śrī Chaitanya-bhāgavata *published by Śrī Caitanya Gauḍīya Maṭha:]*

The one and only object of worship in Kali-yuga is Kṛṣṇa in the mood and complexion of Śrī Rādhā. In other words, His inside is dark in color (*kṛṣṇa*) and His outside is golden (*gaura*). The Supreme Lord Gaurasundara is the combined form of Śrī Rādhā Mādhava. The main way of worshiping

Him is through the mantra consisting of sixteen names and thirty-two syllables.[1]

> "The chanting of the holy names is the way towards salvation in Kali-yuga. For this reason, Śrī Śacīnandana descended to this world. Gauracandra descended for the congregational chanting of the holy names. This is told by the *Śrīmad-Bhāgavatam* and is the essence of all truths."
>
> (*Caitanya-bhāgavata, Ādi-khaṇḍa* 2.22–23)

> "People worshiped the Supreme Lord in Dvāpara-yuga. Various scriptural rules also decree worshiping the Supreme Lord during Kali-yuga. In Kali-yuga, the Supreme Lord descends with a fair complexion and is worshiped by intelligent people through the chanting of His holy names. In this form of Chaitanya Mahāprabhu, He is accompanied by His associates."
>
> (*Śrīmad-Bhāgavatam* 11.5.31–32)

> "The way toward spiritual salvation in Kali-yuga is the congregational chanting of the holy names. Chaitanya Nārāyaṇa broadcasted this message. In order to protect the process of congregational chanting, the Supreme Lord appeared along with all His associates."
>
> (*Caitanya-bhāgavata, Ādi-khaṇḍa* 26–27)

> "The Supreme Lord instructed everyone to hear the *kṛṣṇa-nāma mahā-mantra* with joy: *Hare Kṛṣṇa Hare Kṛṣṇa Kṛṣṇa Kṛṣṇa Hare Hare Hare Rāma Hare Rāma Rāma Rāma Hare Hare*. The Supreme Lord said, 'I have told you the *mahā-mantra*. Go and chant this and you shall attain all perfection. Say this mantra all the time; there are no rules and regulations in this regard.'"
>
> (*Caitanya-bhāgavata, Madhya-khaṇḍa* 23.75–78)

Mahāprabhu gave the garland from His neck to everybody and instructed everyone:

---

1 The mantra referred to here is the Hare Kṛṣṇa *mahā-mantra*: Hare Kṛṣṇa Hare Kṛṣṇa Kṛṣṇa Kṛṣṇa Hare Hare Hare Rāma Hare Rāma Rāma Rāma Hare Hare.

"Go and sing the name of Kṛṣṇa. Say 'Kṛṣṇa,' serve Kṛṣṇa and sing the names of Kṛṣṇa. Don't think anything other than Kṛṣṇa. If anyone has love for Me, then do not sing anything other than the name of Kṛṣṇa. Think of Kṛṣṇa and say His name while lying down, while eating, and while awake."

(*Caitanya-bhāgavata, Madhya-khaṇḍa* 28.25–28)

"That Viṣṇu takes *sannyāsa*, is free from material attachments, one-pointedly fixed on Kṛṣṇa, strongly fixed in the great sacrifice (*mahā-yajña*) of chanting the names of Hari. He is absorbed in ecstatic devotional sentiments, which dispels the devotion-deprived doctrine of the impersonalists."

(*Mahābhārata Sahasra-nāma Stotra*, Verse 75)

"Vṛndāvana dāsa Ṭhākura references this verse of *Mahābhārata* and explains how Veda-vyāsa described the Lord's descent in the form of a *sannyāsī*. The entire community of Vaiṣṇavas knows that the words of Veda-vyāsa came true in the form of the *brāhmaṇa* Viśvambhara."

(*Caitanya-bhāgavata, Madhya-khaṇḍa* 28.166–167)

Vṛndāvana dāsa Ṭhākura's description of Mahāprabhu's *sannyāsa* is unparalleled: "Mahāprabhu was totally unstable when relishing the nectar of transcendental love. He was always overcome with divine ecstasy; He would cry, and His body would tremble. Mahāprabhu's head was shaved while He was in this divine state of ecstasy." According to the *Gauḍīya Bhāṣya*, after taking a bath in the Gaṅgā, Mahāprabhu went to Keśava Bhāratī and first initiated Keśava Bhāratī in the *sannyāsa* mantra and then accepted the mantra from him to teach the general public. Mahāprabhu said:

"I saw a great personality in My dream. He gave Me the *sannyāsa* mantra in My ear. See what it is.' In this way, He told the mantra in the ear of Keśava Bhāratī and made him His disciple. Great wonder came in the mind of Keśava Bhāratī. Bhāratī said, 'This is the great *mahā-mantra*; what is unknown to You?' According to the instruction of Mahāprabhu, Keśava Bhāratī told the mantra to Mahāprabhu.

Then the four directions filled with the sound of the holy names as Mahāprabhu took *sannyāsa.*"

(*Caitanya-bhāgavata, Madhya-khaṇḍa*, 28.155–160)

In this way, Śrīmān Mahāprabhu wore the reddish garments and held a staff in His hand. At the time of performing His *sannyāsa* initiation, Śrī Keśava Bhāratī wondered what name he could give to Mahāprabhu. Although it seemed that Mahāprabhu should have the title Bhāratī, as He was Keśava Bhāratī's disciple, still this name was not necessarily applicable to Him. Śuddha Sarasvatī appeared on Keśava Bhāratī's tongue and said, "You make the world say 'Kṛṣṇa' and thus awaken the consciousness of all. Thus, Your name will be Śrī Kṛṣṇa Chaitanya, as the whole world has become fortunate because of You." Vaiṣṇavas from all four directions filled the environment with the chanting of the holy names and the glories of Mahāprabhu.

Śrīla Kṛṣṇadāsa Kavirāja Gosvāmī has written, "At the end of His twenty-four years of age in the month of Māgha during the waxing moon phase, Mahāprabhu took *sannyāsa.*" (*Caitanya-bhāgavata, Madhya,* 3.3). In *Caitanya-bhāgavata*, Śrīla Vṛndāvana dāsa Ṭhākura has written, "On the day of Uttarāyaṇa Saṅkramaṇa, Mahāprabhu will ascertain that He will take *sannyāsa.*" (*Madhya,* 18.9). Saṅkramaṇa is when the sun enters the beginning of a *rāśi.* When the sun enters the Karkaṭa-rāśi, it is known as Dakṣiṇāyana. When the sun enters the Makara-rāśi, it is known as Uttarāyaṇa. In every solar year, there is one day when the sun enters Dakṣināyaṇa and one day when it enters Uttarāyaṇa. The day when the sun goes from Dhanu-rāśi to Makara-rāśi is known as the Uttarāyaṇa Saṇkramaṇa.

Śrī Gaurasundara made His desire of taking *sannyāsa* known to Śrī Śrī Nityānanda Prabhu, Śrīla Gadādhara Paṇḍita Gosvāmī, Śrīla Chandraśekhara Āchārya, Śrīla Mukunda Datta, and Śrīla Brahmānanda Bhāratī at Chandraśekhara Āchārya's house in Śrīdham Māyāpura. It was in this very place that the Chaitanya Maṭha was established in 1918 and where Śrīla Bhaktisiddhānta Sarasvatī Prabhupāda took *sannyāsa,* following in the footsteps of the Avanti Brāhmaṇa, described in the 11th Canto's 23rd chapter of the *Śrīmad-Bhāgavatam.* Such Vaiṣṇava *sannyāsa* is present in southern India's Rāmānuja *sampradāya* to date. Śrīla Gopāla Bhaṭṭa Gosvāmī has described in the *Hari Bhakti Vilāsa* that he is the disciple of

Prabodhānanda Sarasvatī, who is a *tridaṇḍi sannyāsī* in the Rāmānuja line. Śrīla Sanātana Gosvāmī has written the *Digdarśinī Tīkā* to *Hari Bhakti Vilāsa.* Śrīla Prabodhānanda Sarasvatī was the uncle of Gopāla Bhaṭṭa, as he was the elder brother of Gopāla Bhaṭṭa's father, Veṅkaṭa Bhaṭṭa of Śrī Raṅga-kṣetra. Some people, out of ignorance, think him to be Kāśī's Prakāśānanda Sarasvatī. This is not possible. How can he who was a Rāmānujā *sannyāsī* two years earlier become Kāśī's Māyāvādī *sannyāsī* Prakāśānanda Sarasvatī? This cannot be logically or historically correct. Vṛndāvana dāsa Ṭhākura has explained how Mahāprabhu told the great devotee Murāri Gupta that Māyāvāda is a misguided philosophy bereft of devotion. Śrīla Kavirāja Gosvāmī has also explained how, by the inconceivable mercy of Mahāprabhu, Prakāśānanda Sarasvatī became a devotee. But neither Kavirāja Gosvāmī nor Vṛndāvana dāsa Ṭhākura have explained that Gopāla Bhaṭṭa's *guru*, the author of *Śrī Caitanya-candrāmṛta* and *Śrī Rādhā-rasa-sudhā-nidhi,* and Prakāśānanda Sarasvatī are one and the same.

Many people offend Śrī Nityānanda Prabhu, who is non-different from Baladeva. Vṛndāvana dāsa Ṭhākura has repeated six times, "I kick the head of the sinner who rejects Nityānanda." I am requesting the readers to carefully read the commentaries on these verses by Śrīla Prabhupāda. Nobody other than the devotees can understand that Vṛndāvana dāsa Ṭhākura's apparently harsh words are the greatest compassion. Only when the soul gets the mercy of understanding that one is the eternal servant of the servant of the servant of Kṛṣṇa can one understand the actual humility and respect of Vṛndāvana dāsa Ṭhākura.

Caitanya-bhāgavata, Ādi-khaṇḍa, discusses Mahāprabhu's appearance, childhood, and Gayā *yātrā. Madhya-khaṇḍa* discusses His *kīrtana* pastimes and up to His taking *sannyāsa. Antya-khaṇḍa* then discusses His divine ecstasy in Purī Dhāma. Śrīla Kṛṣṇadāsa Kavirāja Gosvāmī has wholeheartedly glorified Vṛndāvana dāsa Ṭhākura in many parts of his *Caitanya-caritāmṛta.* The devotees of Vṛndāvana were so eager to hear the last pastimes of Mahāprabhu, and after getting the *ājñā-mālā*[2] from Śrī Śrī Rādhā Madanagopāla, Kṛṣṇadāsa Kavirāja Gosvāmī began writing the *Caitanya-caritāmṛta.* He described Vṛndāvana dāsa as the Vyāsadeva of Chaitanya-līlā.

2 An order or instruction (*ājñā*) received in the form of a garland (*mālā*).

In *Caitanya-bhāgavata*, Vṛndāvana dāsa Ṭhākura first glorifies the devotees and states that this glorification is how he knows that his writing of the book will be successful (*Ādi-khaṇḍa* 1.10). The mercy of the Lord follows the mercy of the devotees. "[The Supreme Lord says,] 'One who criticizes My devotees but worships Me and takes My name will have to face obstacles. Those who love My devotees will surely attain Me..... Those who do not worship the devotees of Viṣṇu but worship only Viṣṇu are proud and therefore they do not get the mercy of Viṣṇu." (*Antya-khaṇḍa* 6.95–99)

Vṛndāvana dāsa Ṭhākura then glorifies Nityānanda Prabhu: "All glories to Nityānanda Rāya, through whose mercy the glories of Chaitanya become manifest. Whoever has crossed the ocean of material existence and who is in the ocean of devotion, let them all serve Nitāicānda. Then again, through the mercy of Chaitanya, one gets the mercy of Nityānanda. By knowing Nityānanda, all problems are eliminated." (*Ādi-khaṇḍa* 9.219–220)

At first, *Caitanya-bhāgavata* was known as *Caitanya-maṅgala*. When Locana dāsa Ṭhākura's *Caitanya-maṅgala* began being sung, then Vṛndāvana dāsa Ṭhākura changed the name of his book to *Śrī Caitanya-bhāgavata*. Kavirāja Gosvāmī describes that is it Chaitanya who is speaking through the mouth of Vṛndāvana dāsa Ṭhākura.

Śrīla Prabhupāda has written: "*Śrī Caitanya-bhāgavata* describes the first half of Mahāprabhu's life and the *Caitanya-caritāmṛta* describes the second half. We request the readers to carefully read the *Śrī Caitanya-bhāgavata* in neutrality and after that, the reader will surely be attracted to read the *Caitanya-caritāmṛta*. This is the perfection of the spiritual life of the reader. This is our request to the reader."

I hope that all those desiring eternal auspiciousness will read this book, which presents the essence of the teachings of the *Gītā* and *Bhāgavata* in simple language. It will be the source of happiness for even those who do not have much education.

The descriptions found in the second chapter of the *Ādi-khaṇḍa* and fourth chapter of the *Antya-khaṇḍa* detailing the situation in Navadvīpa prior to the advent of Śrī Chaitanya are worth mentioning: "During this time, people did not understand devotion to Kṛṣṇa. They only desired material gain and were enjoying meat and wine. The environment was in the mode of ignorance. In that society, the acts of the non-Hindus were also frightening and sometimes they would destroy all the temple deities. For example, they destroyed the deities in Odisha. In such a bad time, Mahāprabhu descended and gave fearlessness to everybody: 'Those who offend My devotees and who are intoxicated with knowledge, wealth, high birth, and austerities will be bereft in this age. They will not accept Me. My name will be established in as many villages as there are existing in the world.'"

To respect the pure devotees, Vṛndāvana dāsa Ṭhākura has roared like a lion in some parts of *Caitanya-bhāgavata.* He has greatly spoken against the non-devotional *brāhmaṇa* community. He explained that demons will take birth in *brāhmaṇa* families and that seeing or touching such people is prohibited; on the other hand, Vaiṣṇavas purify the three worlds (*Ādi-khaṇḍa* 300–304). He has also explained how one should be very careful against Vaiṣṇava *aparādha.* One will be bereft of good fortune if he engages in committing offenses against Vaiṣṇavas (*Madhya-khaṇḍa* 22.52). Despite the family a Vaiṣṇava is born in, the Vaiṣṇava is supreme as explained in all scriptures. One who sees a Vaiṣṇava according to his birth will die in low births (*Madhya-khaṇḍa* 10.100, 102).

We ask the readers again and again to read this *Śrī Caitanya-bhāgavata* along with the *Gauḍīya Bhāṣya* commentary of Śrīla Prabhupāda. Through that commentary, the readers will receive great knowledge about pure devotion from the scriptures.

Servant of the servant of the Vaiṣṇavas,
Śrī Bhakti Pramode Purī

Summary Translation of the Introduction to *Śrī Caitanya-caritāmṛta*

by Śrīla Bhakti Pramoda Purī Gosvāmī Ṭhākura

[His Divine Grace Bhakti Pramode Pūri Gosvāmī Ṭhākura has recounted the following anecdotes in his forward to Śri Caitanya-caritāmṛta:*]*

Śrīla Kṛṣṇadāsa Kavirāja Gosvāmī is the celebrated author of *Govinda Līlāmṛta* and the *Śrī Caitanya-caritāmṛta*; but he has given very little information in these books about himself. Despite recent claims that their names have been discovered, no concrete evidence can be found to substantiate them.[3] Kṛṣṇadāsa is a spiritual name, and not one that he used in his family life. Kṛṣṇadāsa has given us some autobiographical information in the fifth chapter of the *Ādi-līlā*, from which we learn that he was born in Jhāmaṭapura, which is near the Salar railway station. He writes in *Caitanya-caritāmṛta*, "There is a village near Naihāṭi named Jhāmaṭapura. Nityānanda Prabhu appeared to me there in a dream." (*Ādi-līlā* 5.181) Śrīla Kṛṣṇadāsa Kaviraj Gosvāmī was ordered to go to Vṛndāvana in a dream by Nityānanda Prabhu. He spent the remainder of his life in Vraja Dhāma.

Regarding the life of Kṛṣṇadāsa Kavirāja Gosvāmī, Śrīla Prabhupāda Sarasvatī Gosvāmī has established Kṛṣṇadāsa's dates by collating information from several sources. He concludes that he was probably born in about 1520 AD and died in about 1616 or 1617. There is some difference of opinion about Kṛṣṇadāsa's caste. Once again, Śrīla Prabhupāda Bhaktisiddhānta Sarasvatī Ṭhākura has discussed this point: "Supporters of different ideas claim that Kṛṣṇadāsa was born in one of the three upper castes (*brāhmaṇa*, *kāyastha* or *vaidya*). Kavirāja is a title given to those who prove themselves by composing literary works that have achieved renown for their quality in learned circles. Since this title is also given to Āyurvedic physicians, some people hold that Kṛṣṇadāsa was a *vaidya*. From this discussion, we can see that Kṛṣṇadāsa may have been born in any of these three castes. Whatever the case, a Vaiṣṇava is superior to a *brāhmaṇa* no matter in what caste he takes his birth. All scriptures state that a Vaiṣṇava is the topmost of all human beings. There is no unanimous opinion about Kṛṣṇadāsa's marital status, either. Some say that he was a lifelong *brahmachārī* when he went to Vṛndāvana. If he had left behind a wife and family, he would likely have mentioned it when telling of his renunciation." Śrīla Prabhupāda writes in this connection, "After arriving in Vṛndāvana, Kṛṣṇadāsa became totally absorbed in *hari-kathā* and indifferent to talk of his previous family life. He was known as Kavirāja Gosvāmī to his spiritual family. His spiritual identity in Vraja-līlā is Ratnarekhā Mañjarī, or Kastūrī Mañjarī according to others."

During his glorification of Nityānanda Prabhu in the *Caitanya-caritāmṛta*, Kṛṣṇadāsa Kavirāja describes a significant event in his life. He had organized

3 According to Ashutosh Deb's Bengali Dictionary and Haridāsa dāsa's *Gauḍīya Vaiṣṇava Abhidhāna*, Kṛṣṇadāsa's parents were named Bhagirath and Sunanda.

a twenty-four-hour *kīrtana* at his house. Amongst those invited was Lord Nityānanda's dear associate Mīnaketana Rāmadāsa, who also lived in Jhāmaṭpura. Mīnaketana was a great Vaiṣṇava who, when he chanted the name of Nityānanda Prabhu, entered a state of devotional trance. While in ecstasy, he would often slap people and sometimes tap them with his flute. In general, his ecstatic behavior was the cause of astonishment amongst Kṛṣṇadāsa Kavirāja's guests and all came to pay their obeisance and offer him respects. Only Mīnaketana Miśra's brother, Guṇārṇava Miśra, who was the *pujārī* of the festival, did not show proper respect to him. This lack of respect indicated that he had no faith in Nityānanda Prabhu. Seeing this, Mīnaketana became very angry and criticized his brother, saying: "Just look! This is a second Romaharṣaṇa Sūta, who did not come forward to show respect when he saw Balarāma!" (*Caitanya-caritāmṛta, Ādi-līlā* 5.170). The Lord is influenced by His devotees, and He gives great importance to even the slightest display of attachment, and seeing such attachment He bestows upon them all that they desire. Kṛṣṇadāsa Kavirāja writes that by taking the side of Nityānanda Prabhu's associate and chastising his brother, he received the blessings of Nityānanda Prabhu himself. Nitāi came to him in a dream and ordered him to go to Vṛndāvana: "O Kṛṣṇadāsa! Have no fear. Go to Vṛndāvana, for there you will attain all things." After saying this, He indicated the way to Vṛndāvana by waving His hand and then disappeared with His associates. (*Caitanya-caritāmṛta, Ādi-līlā* 5.195–6) In contrast to this example of Kṛṣṇadāsa Kavirāja's defense of Nityānanda Prabhu's dear devotee, a person who shows all the customary virtues, yet holds devotees in contempt, is eternally deprived of the Lord's blessings. A good example of this is the *zamindar* Rāmacandra Khān, who committed offenses to Haridāsa Ṭhākura. As a result of this offense, he incurred Nityānanda Prabhu's displeasure.

With words of profound humility, Kṛṣṇadāsa Kavirāja Gosvāmī proclaims the glories of Nityānanda Prabhu:

> "I am more sinful than Jagāi and Mādhāi and lower than a maggot in stool. Whoever hears my name loses the results of his virtuous deeds, and whoever utters my name commits a sin. Other than Nityānanda, could anyone in this world show mercy to one as abominable as me? Nityānanda is the incarnation of mercy; He is so fully intoxicated by

> ecstatic love that He does not discriminate between the good and the bad. He delivers anyone who falls down before Him. Therefore He has delivered such a sinful and fallen person as me."
>
> (*Caitanya-caritāmṛta, Ādi-līlā* 5.205–9)

Without the mercy of Viṣṇu and the Vaiṣṇavas, it is impossible to describe their glories. It is for this reason that Kṛṣṇadāsa Kavirāja Gosvāmī begins each chapter of the *Caitanya-caritāmṛta* with invocations to Mahāprabhu and His associates, like Nityānanda Prabhu and Advaita Ācārya, and concludes each chapter with a prayer for service to the feet of Rūpa and Raghunātha Gosvāmīs. He has thus shown how important it is to avoid any disrespect or offense to the Vaiṣṇavas.

> "Vṛndāvana dāsa is the original biographer of Śrī Chaitanya Mahāprabhu and equal to Śrīla Vyāsadeva, the compiler of all the Vedas. The way he has described Lord Chaitanya's pastimes is very charming and delightful. Afraid that it would become too voluminous, Vṛndāvana dāsa left some pastimes out of his book. I shall try as far as possible to fill in these gaps"
>
> (*Caitanya-caritāmṛta, Ādi-līlā* 13.48–9)

Vrndāvan dāsa Ṭhākura wrote an elaborate outline of Chaitanya Mahāprabhu's *līlā* at the beginning of the *Caitanya-bhāgavata*, but as he became absorbed in describing Nityānanda Prabhu's activities, many pastimes mentioned in the outline were left out of the final version of the book. Mahāprabhu's devotees in Vṛndāvana were afraid that these pastimes would be forgotten and lost forever, so they approached Kṛṣṇadāsa Kavirāja, requesting him to write a complete version of these events. Kṛṣṇadāsa then went to the deity of Madana Mohana and asked for permission to fulfill their desire. In front of all the prominent contemporary members of the Gauḍīya community in Vṛndāvana, Madana Mohana's garland fell from His neck. This was taken by all present as a sign of the Lord's approval and they let out a joyous cheer. Madana Mohana's *pūjāri* picked up the garland and placed it around Kṛṣṇadāsa's neck. Accepting it as a sign of the Deity's desire, Kṛṣṇadāsa Kavirāja began to write the twenty-four thousand *ślokas* of *Caitanya-caritāmṛta* with great humility:

> "*Caitanya-caritāmṛta* is being dictated to me by Madana Mohana. My writing is like the repetition of a parrot. I write as Madana Gopāla orders me, just as a wooden marionette is made to dance by a puppeteer"
>
> (*Caitanya-caritāmṛta, Ādi-līlā* 8.78-9)

> "With the blessings of Śrī Chaitanya Mahāprabhu, although I am an insignificant living being, I have elaborated in writing everything that Svarūpa Dāmodara recorded in his notes about the Lord's pastimes, as well as everything that I heard from the mouth of Raghunātha dāsa."
>
> (*Caitanya-caritāmṛta, Antya-līlā* 3.267-68)

Lord Chaitanya Mahāprabhu's glorious name, form, qualities and activities all manifested in Kṛṣṇadāsa Kavirāja's heart, which he himself confirmed in various places throughout the book:

> "I am now an old man and an invalid. My hand trembles as I write and my memory fails me. I am going blind and deaf, but still I manage to write and this is a great wonder."
>
> (*Caitanya-caritāmṛta, Madhya-līlā* 2.89-90)

Once Śrīla Bhaktisiddhānta Sarasvatī Prabhupāda was glorifying the supremacy of *Caitanya-caritāmṛta* to his disciples, and he instructed them as follows: "If all the books in the world were destroyed, leaving only *Śrīmad-Bhāgavatam* and *Caitanya-caritāmṛta*, then people would still be able to achieve the ultimate goal in life. And even if the *Śrīmad-Bhāgavatam* were lost, leaving only the *Caitanya-caritāmṛta*, there would still be no loss to humanity, for that which has not been revealed in the *Bhāgavatam* is found in *Caitanya-caritāmṛta*. The supreme absolute truth is Śrī Chaitanya Mahāprabhu, the combined form of Rādhā and Kṛṣṇa. The *Caitanya-caritāmṛta* is His sound incarnation."

This statement underscores the special status of Kṛṣṇadāsa Kavirāja Gosvāmī himself. His three books, *Caitanya-caritāmṛta*, *Govinda-līlāmṛta*, and a commentary on *Kṛṣṇa-karṇāmṛta*, are all priceless jewels. *Govinda-līlāmṛta* describes in detail Lord Kṛṣṇa's activities over a twenty-four-hour period. Narottama dāsa Ṭhākura has therefore stated:

kṛṣṇadāsa kavirāja, rasika bhakata mājha
jeṅho kailā caitanya-carita
gaura-govinda-līlā, śunite galaye śilā
tāhāte nā haila mora cita

"Kṛṣṇadāsa Kavirāja Gosvāmī stands out amongst the devotee literati, for he is the author of the biography of Śrī Chaitanya Mahāprabhu. Even the stones melt on hearing his descriptions of Gaura-līlā and Govinda-līlā. Alas, my mind has still not been attracted by these works."
(*Prema-bhakti-candrikā*)

In the illustrious commentary, Viśvanātha Cakravartī's *ṭīkā* to Śrī *Caitanya-caritāmṛta*, we can understand how dear Kṛṣṇadāsa Kavirāja Gosvāmī is to Śrīmatī Rādhārāṇī, and how the deepest and most profound spiritual truths of the divine couple were revealed to him. Every word he wrote is to be taken as the supreme absolute spiritual reality.

"While Viśvanātha Cakravartī was writing his commentary on *Śrī Caitanya-caritāmṛta*, *Madhya-līlā* 21.125, he was unable to understand why Kavirāja Gosvāmī had written that the *kāma-gāyatrī* mantra consists of twenty-four and a half syllables rather than twenty-five. He became so distraught by his inability to comprehend that he finally took a vow to starve to death by the banks of Rādhā-kuṇḍa. As he dozed off in the middle of the night, the daughter of Vṛṣabhānu appeared to him in a dream and said, 'O Viśvanātha! Get up. Kṛṣṇadāsa has indeed written correctly. He is my dear associate, who brings me much pleasure. I have blessed him so that he can understand the most intimate things about me. Do not doubt anything he has written. In the book named *Varṇāgama-bhāsvata*, it is written that whenever the syllable *ya* is followed by the syllable *vi*, it is considered to be only half a syllable.'"

In the *Bhakti-ratnākara* it is mentioned that Śrīnivasa Ācārya met Kṛṣṇadāsa Kavirāja, Raghunātha dāsa Gosvāmī and Śrī Rāghava when he arrived in Vṛndāvana (*Bhakti-ratnākara* 4.392).

On the grounds of Kṛṣṇadāsa Kavirāja's home in Jhāmaṭapura is a small temple containing Nityānanda's footprints. Local legend has it that Kṛṣṇadāsa Kavirāja received Nityānanda's mercy, i.e., mantra initiation, at this very spot. According to the *Prema-vilāsa*, however, Kṛṣṇadāsa took initiation from Raghunātha dāsa Gosvāmī. In the temple, there is a wooden sandal that is said to have belonged to Kṛṣṇadāsa Kavirāja. His *bhajana kuṭīra* and *samādhi* tomb are in Rādhā-kuṇḍa. He disappeared after Raghunātha dāsa Gosvāmī, on the exact same *tithi*, Śuklā Dvādaśī in the month of Āśvina.

Vṛndāvana dāsa Ṭhākura's Life History

From the Introduction to Śrī Caitanya-bhāgavata
by Śrīla Bhaktisiddhānta Sarasvatī Ṭhākura Prabhupāda

There is an old settlement still present today at Māmagāchi, which is in Pūrvasthalī, Burdwan, West Bengal. The ancient people and the writer of *Bhakti Ratnākara* have said that this place is within the island of Modadrumadvīpa. The Bhāgīrathī river is located at the end of Māmagāchi. The Gaura Nitāī deities of Vṛndāvana dāsa Ṭhākura are served up to the present day in this village. It is heard that Ṭhākura Vṛndāvana took birth in this village. His home there is identified as the place where he spent his childhood.

The parental home of Mālinī, the wife of Śrīvasa Ṭhākura, is present in Māmagāchi. Śrīvasa Ṭhākura was very dear to Mahāprabhu. His brother's daughter, Nārāyaṇī, was married in Māmagāchi village. In her last days, Mālinī Devī came to stay in her father's home. Nārāyaṇī was married to somebody from this family lineage. Śrī Vṛndāvana dāsa was born from the womb of Nārāyaṇī Devī. Vṛndāvana dāsa Ṭhākura's father died when Vṛndāvana dāsa was a child and before he became involved in the service of Mahāprabhu. As a result, his name is not found anywhere. Some say that since he was not completely devoted to Hari, he was not connected with Vṛndāvana dāsa. Although there is little information about Vṛndāvana dāsa Ṭhākura's paternal family, scholars recognize that he was a Rāḍha *brāhmaṇa*. Moreover, he is known as the son of his mother's side of the family, a family who were one-pointedly surrendered to Mahāprabhu.

Śrī Vṛndāvana dāsa Ṭhākura stayed at Denur for a long time. There is no information suggesting he married. Of his four disciples, one was Rāmahari, who was a Kāyastha from Northern Rāḍha. Vṛndāvana dāsa Ṭhākura made him the recipient of all his property at Denur. The familial descendants of Rāmahari are staying at this holy place of Vṛndāvana dāsa Ṭhākura and performing the services there. Although Rāmahari took proper initiaiton, his descendants were influenced by the *smārta* traditions of the time and eventually gave up some proper scriptural etiquettes.

Ṭhākura Vṛndāvana was very proficient in the devotional scriptures. Being fixed in Vaiṣṇava etiquette, he devoted his body, mind, and words to the service of spreading the glories of the Vaiṣṇava spiritual masters. The *smārta* society which was against the Vaiṣṇavas did not like Nityānanda Prabhu. As a result, Vṛndāvana dāsa Ṭhākura, who was Nityānanda's servant, was not kept in a high position by the *smārta* society. They also did not fail to spread false information about Vṛndāvana dāsa Ṭhākura.

A few years before Śri Gaurasundara took *sannyāsa* and left Navadvīpa, Ṭhākura Mahāśaya's mother, Nārāyaṇī, was only a four-year-old child. At that time, she was the recipient of great affection from Mahāprabhu. Thereafter, she was married to someone in the familial lineage of Mālinī Devī and took care of Vṛndāvana dāsa Ṭhākura throughout his childhood. Some *prākṛta-sahajiyās* of the *smārta brāhmaṇa* community of Rāḍha, who were fake Vaiṣṇavas, started to see her as an outsider. While he deserved the topmost position of the *brāhmaṇa* community, Vṛndāvana dāsa Ṭhākura did not become subordinate to the *smārta* society, a society which was opposed to spiritual development. Those who have read the *Śrī Caitanya-bhāgavata* of this great author know that he is the supreme protector of the path of pure devotion manifested by Śrī Chaitanyacandra. Vṛndāvana dāsa Ṭhākura had protested much of the *smārta* ideals that entered society at that time. Then again, those *smārta* people could not stop Vṛndāvana dāsa Ṭhākura from presenting the truth in his *Caitanya-bhāgavata*. Those who read *Śrī Caitanya-bhāgavata* cannot be put onto the wrong path.

In this book, Śrīla Vṛndāvana dāsa Ṭhākura presented the wonderful societal conciliation of devotional truths. His service inclination towards his *gurudeva*, Nityānanda, is incomparable. No scholar of the world, whether from India, Bengal, or Navadvīpa, could touch Vṛndāvana dāsa Ṭhākura. Yet, in the time thereafter, when people were trying to defame him, they did not hesitate to attack his birth lineage or his personal mood.

There is no dearth of people ready to attack Śrī Ṭhākura Mahāśaya's great qualities. Some, who harbour animosity towards Vaiṣṇavas, say that by displaying utter dislike for those who are not Vaiṣṇavas, Ṭhākura Mahāśaya and his eternal followers have become incapable of attracting the uninformed with the beauty of Śrī Gaura's example of tolerance and the dharma of humility. In response to that, Vṛndāvana dāsa Ṭhākura's followers say that the animosity fomented by these vile, *bhakti*-inimical persons as they mislead people by making these sorts of critiques, all while mounting their thrones of righteousness in the garb of great authorities of literature, is simply indicative of their own misfortune. When one lacks pious merits, then one can be disobedient to spiritual masters and Vaiṣṇavas. Śrī Ṭhākura Mahāśaya is totally absorbed in service to Guru Nityānanda. Therefore, Śrī Chaitanya did not permit litterateurs and ignorant, righteous people to find fault with Ṭhākura Mahāśaya. When these criticizers desist from dancing to their own whims on the platform of the six enemies of the heart, then they will be able to see Śrī Ṭhākura Mahāśaya as the one and only spiritual master of the Gauḍīyas and begin to repent for the offenses they committed against him, who is their own spiritual master.

The writing of *Śrī Caitanya-bhāgavata* is very clear and heartwarming. The various topics, such as Haridāsa Ṭhākura's narrative, the situation at the time of Gauranga's birth, the *brāhmaṇas*' opinion on chanting the holy names, the narrative of Gaurasundara's opulence and glories, and so on, as so efficiently described by Ṭhākura Mahāśaya, will make this book gain great glory amongst the works of famous litterateurs. Those wishing to enter the temple of literature will be able to see a devotional literature apart from the illusory sense gratifying literature. Gauḍīya people are not only the people from Bengal. They use the language of Bengal and gain expertise in the language of those liberated associates of the Lord in Goloka to be known as Gauḍīyas along with God.

I have finished my writing by quoting from the writing of our predecessor *gurudeva*, Śrīla Kavirāja Gosvāmī, in his *Śrī Caitanya-caritāmṛta*:

Offering of Śrī Kavirāja Gosvāmī to Vṛndāvana dāsa Ṭhākura

O foolish people, listen to the *Caitanya-maṅgala*. You will know all the glories of Chaitanya from it. Veda-vyāsa wrote the pastimes of Kṛṣṇa in the *Bhāgavata*. The Vyāsa of Chaitanya-līlā is Vṛndāvana dāsa. Vṛndāvana dāsa wrote the *Caitanya-maṅgala*. All inauspiciousness is destroyed by hearing that *Caitanya-maṅgala*. One will know the glories of Chaitanya and Nitāī. The conclusion of the devotion to Kṛṣṇa shall be known. He has written all the devotional conclusions from the *Bhāgavata*, herein. If a fallen person or Muslim hears the *Caitanya-maṅgala*, then he will become the greatest Vaiṣṇava, then and there. A human being cannot write such a book. Śrī Chaitanya has spoken through the words of Vṛndāvana dāsa. Ten million obeisances to Vṛndāvana dāsa's feet. He delivered the material world by writing such a book. Nārāyaṇī ate the remnants of Śrī Chaitanya. Śrī dāsa Vṛndāvana came from her womb. What a wonderful description of the pastimes of Chaitanya he wrote! By hearing it, the three worlds became purified. Vṛndāvana dāsa wrote the *Caitanya-maṅgala* wherein he described all the pastimes of Chaitanya in short. Then, he expanded upon the writing. Seeing the length, he felt some hesitation and then did not describe some pastimes. He was overcome writing the pastimes of Nityānanda. Some pastimes of Chaitanya were left over. I meditate on the lotus feet of Vṛndāvana dāsa. Taking his permission, I write that which is auspicious. Chaitanya-līlā's Vyāsa is Vṛndāvana dāsa. Nothing else can be manifested without his mercy. Vṛndāvana dāsa is the son of Nārāyaṇī. He wrote the *Caitanya-maṅgala*. Veda-vyāsa described the pastimes of Kṛṣṇa in the *Bhagavata*. The Vyāsa of Chaitanya-līlā is Vṛndāvana dāsa. Chaitanya-līlā's Vyāsa is Vṛndāvana dāsa. He described the pastimes very sweetly. Chaitanya-līlā's Vyāsa is dāsa Vṛndāvana. I write that which is left over from his writings, taking his permission...

Siddhānta Sarasvatī

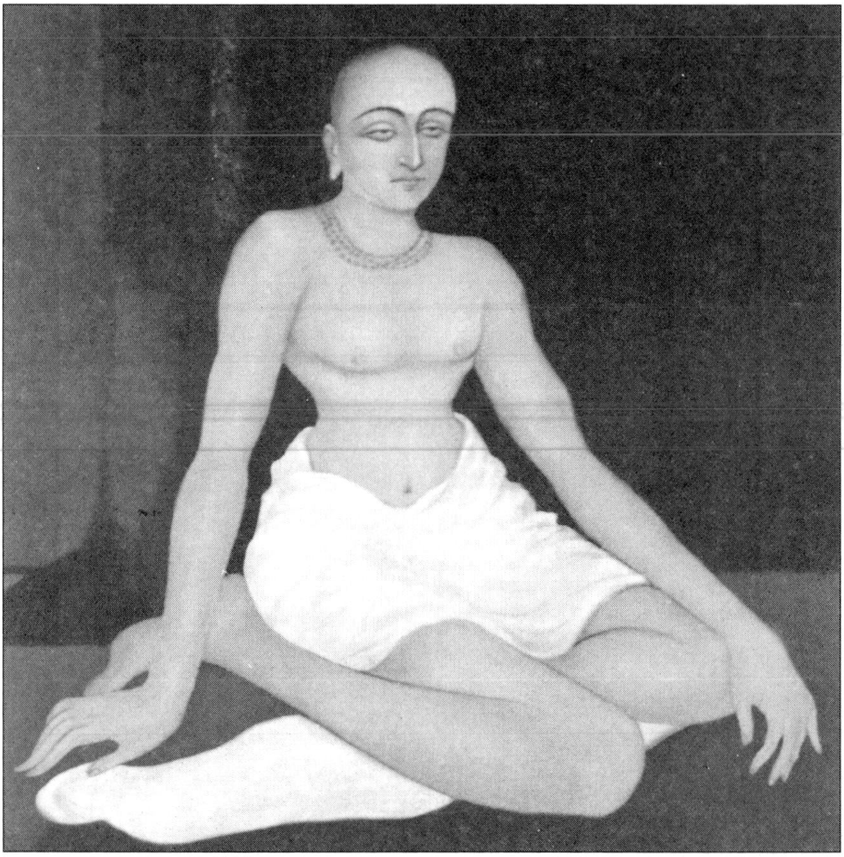

Part I
Early Life

The Soul's States of Existence

At the time of Śrī Chaitanya Mahāprabhu's appearance, the earth was suffering from high turbulence due to casteism and racism and was dominated by cruel rulers of demoniac character, whose actions were inhumane and irreligious. There was a great deal of violence and living a peaceful life was next to impossible. *Brāhmaṇas* and other upper castes in society, whom the people would normally look to for leadership and guidance, instead created and forced on others religious practices for selfish motives and pseudo asceticism. Thus, people were extremely distressed. To maintain their livelihood, they had no choice but to follow these sinful principles promoted in the name of religion. With no option left, the people were in despair. They begged for mercy from the Supreme Lord and prayed for shelter at His lotus feet. Would there be any hope for them?

Śrī Kṛṣṇa is the Supreme Lord. One of His plenary expansions is Saṅkarṣaṇa, and one of Saṅkarṣaṇa's plenary expansions is Kāraṇodakaśāyī Mahā-Viṣṇu. When Kāraṇodakaśāyī Mahā-Viṣṇu looks at the illusory energy, *māyā*, this glance causes the creation of the material world. Various types of *jīvas* are present in the material world due to being bound by their previous actions. This state of the *jīvas* (living entities) being bound in illusion due to previous actions is known as being *māyābaddha*. How many states of existence exist for a *māyābaddha jīva*? We are informed of the answers to these questions by our most worshipful Śrī Śrīmad Bhaktivinoda Ṭhākura.

A *māyābaddha jīva* has five states of consciousness. In other words, according to the *jīva's* materially bound state, its consciousness is covered (*ācchādita-cetana*), shrunken (*saṅkucita-cetana*), budding (*mukulita-cetana*), blooming (*vikasita-cetana*), or blossomed (*pūrṇa-vikasita-cetana*). Now let us discuss these five states of consciousness according to the classifications provided by Śrī Śrīmad Bhaktivinoda Ṭhākura:

(1) Covered Consciousness (*ācchādita-cetana*) – Trees, grass, stones, rocks, and mountains are all living entities who possess completely covered-over consciousness. Their understanding of *dharma* is practically nonexistent and is considered to be in a sleeping state. Having forgotten their constitutional existence of being the servants of Kṛṣṇa, they are so deeply absorbed in the qualities of material nature that they have absolutely no cognizance of their eternal spiritual existence in the spiritual world. Through the six transformations of the body (*ṣaḍ-vikāra*), they possess a slight understanding of their true existence. This is the most fallen state of existence of the *jīva*. When one discusses the Purāṇic histories of Ahalyā, Yamalārjuna trees, Saptātala, and so on, it is seen that one attains this state of completely covered-over consciousness due to committing an extremely heinous offense. One becomes delivered from such a state of existence by Kṛṣṇa's mercy.

(2) Shrunken Consciousness (*saṅkucita-cetana*) – Animals, birds, reptiles, aquatics (like fish), and insects all possess a shrunken consciousness. Those with a covered consciousness have practically no realization of anything. In comparison, living entities with a shrunken consciousness have a somewhat higher level of realization and understanding. They act according to their desires in regard to gathering food, sleeping, and defending. They can dispute with others in order to maintain their own existence. They become angry upon seeing injustice. All these qualities are seen in one with a shrunken consciousness. They do not have any knowledge of the spiritual world. Even a monkey possessing evil intelligence exhibits some sort of reasoning capability. They think about what will happen in the

future if an action is performed now and so on. Signs of gratitude can be seen in their mindsets. A knowledge of food quality and value is also clearly seen in some of these creatures. Those with a shrunken consciousness do not try to find out about the Supreme Lord. Thus, their understanding of *dharma* is narrow. Bhakta Bharata, despite receiving the body of a deer, possessed knowledge of the Supreme Lord and His name. While this pastime has been described in the scriptures, it is a unique example; it is certainly not the norm. Due to his offense, Bharata had to take birth in the animal kingdom. By the mercy of the Supreme Lord, after committing an offense, Bharata was reestablished on the proper path towards attaining the Lord.

(3) – (5) Budding, Blooming and Blossomed Consciousness (*mukulita, vikasita* and *pūrṇa-vikasita-cetana*) – A bound soul (*baddha-jīva*) is seen to be in three states of existence, namely: the budding state of consciousness (*mukulita-avasthā*), the blooming state of consciousness (*vikasita-avasthā*), and the blossomed state of consciousness (*pūrṇa-vikasita-avasthā*). Humans can be classified into five categories. Those who follow no rules (*nīti-śunya*), those who follow rules but do not believe in a supreme controller (*nirīśvara naitika*), those who do follow rules and do believe in a supreme controller (*seśvara naitika*), those who perform devotional practices in a regulated manner (*sādhana-bhakta*) and those who are in the initial stages of loving devotion (*bhāva-bhakta*). Humans who, due to ignorance or due to changes in knowledge, do not believe in a supreme controller are classified as either *nīti-śunya* or *nirīśvara naitika*. Those who follow rules and have some belief in a supreme controller are known as *seśvara naitika*. Those who engage in devotional practices according to the rules and regulations mentioned in the scriptures are known as *sādhana-bhaktas*. Those who have attained the initial stages of love in relation to the Supreme Lord are known as *bhāva-bhaktas*. The *nīti-śunya* and *nirīśvara naitika* are in the budding stage (*mukulita*). The *seśvara naitika* and the *sādhana-bhakta* are in the blooming stage (*vikasita*). The *bhāva-bhakta* is in the blossomed stage (*pūrṇa-vikasita*).

According to the above mentioned analysis of Śrī Śrīmad Bhaktivinoda Ṭhākura Mahāśaya, the Supreme Lord, Śrī Kṛṣṇa, has sent the *jīva* in a human body, which is the greatest body amongst the Lord's creation, to the material world, completely equipped to attain a blossomed (*pūrṇa-vikasita*) state of consciousness. It is impossible for a *jīva* to attain this blossomed state of conscious through its individual effort. Therefore, a person must first take shelter of the lotus feet of a genuine spiritual master (*sadguru-padāśraya*). The true meaning of taking the shelter of the lotus feet of a genuine spiritual master is as follows: spiritual teachings come down through the generations from spiritual master to disciple through the *guru-paramparā*. When such teachings reach a living entity through the initiating spiritual master (*dīkṣā-guru*) and instructing spiritual masters (*śikṣā-guru*), we must accept those teachings from the cores of our hearts and proceed accordingly on our spiritual paths. The initiating spiritual master (*dīkṣā-guru*) is capable of doing the work of an instructing spiritual master (*śikṣā-guru*). In the absence of the initiating spiritual master (*dīkṣā-guru*), in accordance with his instructions, one can accept one or more instructing spiritual masters (*śikṣā-gurus*). The instructions from the initiating and instructing spiritual masters gradually cause an increase in our strength to perform our spiritual practice (*sādhana-bala*). This *sādhana-bala* is our assistant in achieving the state of a blossomed consciousness (*pūrṇa-vikasita*).

The Birth of Śrī Chaitanya

When the entire society was in tremendous turbulence, the land of Bengal was blessed with the appearance of a great luminary on February 18, 1486. Śrī Chaitanya Mahāprabhu, prophesized as the incarnation of divine love by the Vedic scriptures, was born in a *brāhmaṇa* family in the town of Navadvīpa, West Bengal, India. Throughout His life, acquaintances affectionately referred to Him by many names, such as Śacī-nandana, the son of Śacī, His mother. Because His birth took place under a neem tree, He was also lovingly called Nimāī, especially during His childhood and youth. The townspeople knew Him as Gaurāṅga because of His light, golden skin and physical beauty. Later in life, upon taking vows of renunciation, He would formally be given the name Kṛṣṇa Chaitanya, and after His reputation as a great saint spread, the honorific title Mahāprabhu (great master) was further bestowed upon Him.

Chaitanya's forefathers came from Sylhet in East Bengal but had left their ancestral home to come to Navadvīpa, which was then a great center of learning. They established the new family home on the banks of the Ganges, where Chaitanya's father, Jagannātha Miśra, had been born. Chaitanya's mother, Śacī, was the eldest daughter of another Navadvīpa scholar, the astrologer Nīlāmbara Cakravartī. The young couple had eight successive daughters, but none survived childbirth. Finally, Śacī's ninth child, a boy named Viśvarūpa, was born. Twelve years later, Chaitanya followed.

Chaitanya's birth corresponded with Kṛṣṇa's spring swing festival, Dol Yātrā, which is celebrated on the full-moon day between February and March. Vaiṣṇava theologians say that Kṛṣṇa, who is always absorbed in the love of His precious *gopīs*, accepted the mood and golden hue of the goddess Rādhārāṇī and left His beloved Vṛndāvana to appear in His secret abode of Navadvīpa, the hidden Vṛndāvana. In this incarnation, He flooded the land of Bengal with divine love and brought order back into the land's political, judicial, and social orders.

Ordinarily, on the full-moon day, the moon proudly rises to bathe the world in pure, gentle rays of silver. On the Dol Pūrṇimā of 1486, however, there was an eclipse, as though nature was announcing that another moon, unique and divine, was also rising on that night—one that was greater in fullness, purity, coolness, gentleness, generosity, and poetic beauty than any ordinary moon, or indeed any other joy-giving thing in the world. As it was spring, the still leafless trees were filled with fresh new twigs and copper-colored sprouts. The mango buds were attracting swarms of buzzing bees in search of nectar, while the flower shrubs and creepers waved their branches and spread their fragrance in the wind. It was as though the goddess of nature herself was a young bride who, on hearing the jingling ankle bells of her groom, the Lord of the infinite worlds, had dressed herself in all her finery and was now eagerly awaiting His arrival for the wedding. Seeing nature take on such a beautiful aspect, one could easily conclude that this truly was the day that the Creator and His creation were to be united.

The ladies of the town blew their conch shells, filling the earth and sky with an auspicious reverberation. In every direction, the earth was filled with peace; the river waters were calm and even the ordinary plants and creatures seemed to be filled with joy. The world was awash with bliss. The sound of the Supreme Lord's name was on everyone's lips and all hearts overflowed with happiness. It was as though all were holding their breath in expectation of His appearance as Nimāī, the son of Śacī.

jagat bhariyā loka bale — 'hari' 'hari'
sei-kṣaṇe gaurakṛṣṇa bhūme avatari
(*Caitanya-caritāmṛta, Ādi-līlā* 13.94)

"At the very moment the world was filled with the sound of people everywhere calling out the names of God [in response to the eclipse], Kṛṣṇa descended to the earth in His golden form."

kali-kāle nāma-rūpe kṛṣṇa-avatāra
nāma haite haya sarva-jagat-nistāra
(*Caitanya-caritāmṛta, Ādi-līlā* 17.22)

"Kṛṣṇa appears in this age of Kali in the form of His name. This entire universe will be saved by chanting the names of God."

nāma vinu kali-kāle nāhi āra dharma
sarva-mantra-sāra nāma, ei śāstra-marma
(*Caitanya-caritāmṛta, Ādi-līlā* 7.74)

"There is no religious practice in this age of Kali other than the chanting of the holy names. The holy names are the essence of all mantras—this is the fundamental meaning of all the scriptures."

After the mother gives birth to the child, she is considered impure for twenty-one days. During that time, she stays in the room where she gave birth to her child. After those twenty-one days, the mother comes out with the baby and performs the worship of various gods and goddesses. This day is known as the *niṣkramaṇa-līlā*. Śacī Mātā came out of the room after twenty-one days and performed worship of Gaṅgā Devī and Ṣaṣṭhī Devī. The baby who was commonly known as Nimāī was crying and would only stop when everybody would chant the holy names of Hari. In this way, Śacī Devī's house became constantly filled with the chanting of the holy names of Kṛṣṇa.

Nimāī's Name-giving Ceremony

After Chaitanya's birth, Nīlāmbara Cakravartī assessed the birth chart of the child. Nīlāmbara Cakravartī saw that this child was the Supreme Lord, Nārāyaṇa, and that He would establish the essence of all Vedic spiritual principles in the world. Furthermore, the chart assessed that the boy's preaching would be most wonderful and that He would deliver the whole world. He would make that which Brahmā, Śiva, Śukadeva Gosvāmī, and other exalted personalities desire to obtain easily accessible to all. Nīlāmbara Cakravartī also explained how the living entities who would see this child would then develop compassion towards all souls, would become indifferent towards material happiness and sadness, and would develop love for Gaura-Kṛṣṇa. Even Muslims and people who have enmity towards Lord Viṣṇu would serve the divine lotus feet of this boy. All the innumerable universes would glorify this child and everyone from the lowest of births up to the highest *brāhmaṇas* would offer their obeisance to Him; His glories would make everyone blissful.

Nīlāmbara Cakravartī saw that the boy's body was imbued with the essence of the principles of the *Śrīmad-Bhāgavatam*. He concluded that, in accordance with the scriptures, the name Viśvambhara was appropriate, for it means one who supports, nourishes, and protects (*bhara*) the universe (*viśvam*). He also said that the people would call the child the moon of Navadvīpa – Navadvīpa-candra. Nīlāmbara Cakravartī could see from the horoscope that this child would take the vow of renunciation (*sannyāsa*) in the future, but he did not reveal this to the parents so as not cause them any sadness on this joyous occasion.

Jagannātha Miśra, hearing the future of his child, became overwhelmed in bliss and wanted to give so much in charity to the astrologer. However, due to his poor financial condition, he did not have anything to give. Jagannātha Miśra held the divine feet of the astrologer and cried; in reciprocation, the astrologer caught hold of the divine feet of Jagannātha Miśra and cried as well. All the people present were in bliss and chanted, "Hari! Hari!" Everybody who heard the predictions from the horoscope became blissful and said, "All glories! All glories!" and so made the atmosphere auspicious. All the gods and goddesses appeared disguised as normal men and women and blessed the child by touching His head with paddy and *dūrvā* grass; they gave best wishes that the child would live long. They also offered their obeisance to Śacī Mātā. The goddesses all took the dust from Śacī Mātā's divine feet and place it on their heads. All the while, musicians were playing various musical instruments like *mṛdaṇga* (clay drums), shehnai, and *vaṁśi* (flutes).

Although the scriptures inform us that the Supreme Lord Śrī Kṛṣṇa is the spiritual master of the entire universe (*jagat-guru*), the main object of worship in the Gauḍīya Matha is Śrīmatī Rādhārāṇī. Śrī Kṛṣṇa Chaitanya Mahāprabhu is Kṛṣṇa who has taken on the mood and complexion of Śrīmatī Rādhārāṇī. The scriptures inform us that the Supreme Lord Śrī Kṛṣṇa appears in one day of Brahmā during the Kali-yuga of the twenty-eighth *catura-yuga* in the seventh *manvantara* as Śrī Kṛṣṇa Chaitanya Mahāprabhu. Through His own behavior and activities and having taken upon the mood of Śrīmatī Rādhāraṇī, He gives us the teachings of serving Śrī Kṛṣṇa. At present, some people, without knowing scriptural evidence, accept Śrī Kṛṣṇa Chaitanya Mahāprabhu (Śrī Gaurāṅga Mahāprabhu) to be that same Śrī Kṛṣṇa who performs pastimes and wanders about in the supreme spiritual abode of Goloka Vṛndāvana. Below, I have provided some scriptural verses as evidence for such people regarding this topic:

ajāyadhavamajāyadhavamajāyamadhavaṁ na saṁśaya
kalau saṁkīrtanārambhe bhaviṣyāmi śacīsutaḥ
(*Bhaviṣyapurāṇaḥ*)

"In the age of Kali, I will appear as the son of Śacī Devī to begin the *saṅkīrtana* movement. There is no doubt of this."

kalighoratamasācchannān sarvānācāra varjitan
śacīgarbhe ca saṃbhūya tāriyiṣyāmi nārada
(*Vāmanapurāṇaḥ*)

"O, Nārada! I will take birth from the womb of Śacī Devī to deliver all the people who are bereft of proper conduct and who are overcome by the darkness of the horrible age of Kali."

kaleḥ prathamasandhyāyāṁ lakṣmīkāntobhaviṣyati
brahmarūpaṁ samāśritya sambhavāmi yuge yuge
(*Varāhapurāṇaḥ*)

"In the first portion of the age of Kali, I will appear as the beloved of Lakṣmī and subsequently, will take shelter of Jagannātha. Like this, I appear age after age."

golokanca parityaktvā lokānāṁ trāṇakāriṇām
kalau gaurāṅga-rūpeṇa līlālāvaṇya vigrahaṁ
(*Mārkaṇḍeyapurāṇaḥ*)

"In order to deliver the people of the material world, I will give up My residence of Goloka and take on the form of Gaurāṅga, in the age of Kali, performing beautiful pastimes in My enchanting form."

kaleḥ prathamasandhyāyāṁ gaurāṅgo'saumahītale
bhāgīrathītaṭebhūmni bhaviṣyati sanātana
(*Padmapurāṇaḥ*)

"The eternal Lord, Gaurāṅga, will appear in the first portion of the age of Kali on earth by the banks of the Ganges River."

bhaktiyoga pradānāya lokasyānugrahāya ca
sannyāsirūpamāśritya kṛṣṇaChaitanya nāmadhṛk
(*Bṛhat-vāmanapurāṇaḥ*)

"The Supreme Lord will take *sannyāsa* and will be known as Śrī Kṛṣṇa Chaitanya; He will appear to distribute the yoga of devotion and to bless the people of the world."

gopālaṁ paripālayan vrajapure lokān vahan dvāpare
gauraṅga-priyakīrtanaḥ kaliyuge Chaitanyanāmā hariḥ
(*Nṛsiṁhapurāṇaḥ*)

"The Supreme Lord, Gopāla, who appeared in the age of Dvāpara in Vraja to carry the burden of the earth appears in the age of Kali with the name of Chaitanya in a golden form, lovely chanting the holy names of Hari."

After reading the above quotes, I hope that there are no doubts in the minds of the readers regarding Śrī Kṛṣṇa Chaitanya Mahāprabhu being the Supreme Lord Śrī Kṛṣṇa Himself.

Throughout His childhood and youth, everyone continued to affectionately call Him Nimāī. He was born under the neem tree and His mother's nickname was Āī; thus, He got the nickname "Nimāī." He also had other names according to His qualities. He was golden in color, so people used to call Him Gaura, Gaurāṅga, Gaurahari, Gaurasundara, and Gauragopāla. He was also known as Śacī-nandana and Jagannātha-sūta because He was the son of Mother Śacī and Father Jagannātha Miśra.

Nimāī's First Grains

Six months after birth, Nimāī was fed His first grains as per Brahmanical traditions. Before feeding the child grains, there is a test of taste known as a *ruci-parīkṣa*. Paddy (*dhaan*), parched rice (*khoi*), silver, gold, seashells, a book, and a pen were placed on a plate. When the plate was placed in front of Nimāī, He chose the book, meaning that He would be a great scholar and follow the *Śrīmad-Bhāgavatam*, which represents pure devotion. After completing this portion of the ceremony, He was fed His first grains.

Thereafter, Nimāī started crawling. He used to crawl everywhere. He would try to catch whatever was in front of Him. When there was fire in front of Him, Nimāī would go and try to catch the fire. When there was a snake in front of Him, He would go to catch the snake. The elders would always try to protect Him from these dangers. Whenever Nimāī would cry, He would only stop crying when the surrounding devotees would clap their hands and chant the holy names of Hari. Once, Nimāī was crawling in the courtyard and a big snake appeared in the courtyard. Nimāī quickly went and caught the snake. The snake then coiled up and Nimāī lay on the coils of the snake. Actually, that snake was Ananta-deva Saṅkarṣaṇa, who wanted to serve Gaura Nārāyaṇa in His childhood pastimes. Nimāī's parents and relatives thought that it was an ordinary snake and tried to release Nimāī from the snake by praying to Garuḍa, the eagle carrier of Lord Viṣṇu. They were crying out of fear. Then, the snake just slithered away, but Nimāī was crawling and trying to catch the snake. Actually, no one understood that Nimāī is not an ordinary boy; nobody knew that He was non-different from Kṛṣṇa. Their parental love was so strong that Nimāī's godliness was covered over. The elders picked up Nimāī in their arms and began chanting auspicious mantras and invocations to protect Nimāī from any danger.

As Nimāī started growing up, He looked so beautiful and had mystical qualities. He would sometimes laugh and sometimes cry because He wanted the moon. In the early mornings, most of the neighbors would come to see Nimāī. They used to surround Him and chant the holy names while clapping their hands. Nimāī's body was decorated with gold, silver, jewels, and many beautiful ornaments. One day, two thieves saw all the beautiful jewels on Nimāī's body and became greedy to steal the ornaments. One of the thieves gave Nimāī a sweetmeat (*sandeśa*) and took Him onto his shoulders and began walking on the streets of Navadvīpa town. They went some distance away from Nimāī's home and started splitting up the ornaments between each other. At home, everyone was crying loudly as they couldn't find Nimāī. Then, they took shelter of Govinda. Meanwhile, the thieves became bewildered and thought that they were taking Nimāī to their home; little did they realize that they had arrived back at the home of Jagannātha Miśra. Nimāī saw His parents and climbed into His father's arms. Everyone became so blissful. The thieves thought, "What's this? Where have we come? Is this a miracle or what?" Amid the crowd at Jagannātha Miśra's home, the two thieves escaped, thinking, "We have been stealing for a long time, but we never faced such a dangerous situation. By our good fortune, Caṇḍī Mātā has protected us. We must offer Her a good *pūjā*." Jagannātha Miśra began looking for who had brought Nimāī but couldn't find any sign of anybody. However, the thieves were very fortunate, as they had carried Nimāī, who is the Supreme Lord, on their shoulders.

Symbols on His Divine Feet

One day, Jagannātha Miśra called Nimāī to bring a book from his room. Nimāī happily went to bring the book to fulfill the desire of Jagannātha Miśra. As soon as they heard the sound of ankle bells, both Jagannātha Miśra and Śacī Mātā thought, "Where is the sound coming from? Nimāī is not wearing any ankle bells." They were not able to speak and were wondering what was going on. Nimāī came and gave the book to his father and went to play. After that, the parents saw the entire floor filled with the signs that are present on the feet of the Supreme Lord, namely: a flag, goad, lightning bolt, thunderbolt, and various other symbols. Both parents were so happy seeing these signs on the floor that their eyes filled with tears; they were in ecstasy. Seeing the divine feet symbols, they offered their obeisance and thought that they would have no more births in the material world. Then, Jagannātha Miśra told Śacī Mātā to prepare sweet rice with clarified butter. They surmised that the Dāmodara *śālagrāma* had come walking in their house. However, they could not realize that the footprints with divine symbols were Nimāī's. When they were worshiping the *śālagrāma*, Nimāī was laughing in His mind as He knew what had taken place.

Visit from a Wandering Mendicant

One day, a *brāhmaṇa* who used to travel to various holy places came to Jagannātha Miśra's house. He had his *śālagrāma-śilā* deity in a pouch hanging from his neck down to his chest. Jagannātha Miśra welcomed the *brāhmaṇa* very lovingly. This *brāhmaṇa* would daily cook a fresh meal, offer it to his Bāla-gopāla *śālagrāma* deity, and then honor those remnants. He never used to eat anything else. Jagannātha Miśra brought all the rice, *dāl*, and vegetables that the *brāhmaṇa* would need to cook. The *brāhmaṇa* graciously accepted the ingredients, cooked the meal, kept it in front of his deity, and sat in meditation, offering the food to the *śālagrāma*. When the *brāhmaṇa* was in meditation, little Nimāī came running and ate the rice. The *brāhmaṇa* opened his eyes and saw that Nimāī was standing in front of him, eating the offering that he had cooked for Bāla-gopāla. Jagannātha Miśra came running to chastise Nimāī but the *brāhmaṇa* forbade him to do so, saying that maybe it was the Lord's wish that he eat only fruits and roots that day. Jagannātha Miśra begged the *brāhmaṇa* to please cook one more time for his Bāla-gopāla *śālagrāma*.

After Jagannātha Miśra's sincere pleading, the *brāhmaṇa* agreed to cook again. He cooked the rice and vegetables, kept them in front of his deity, and sat down in meditation, offering the cooking to his Bāla-gopāla. This time, Nimāī arrived and laughingly took a fistful of rice and ate it. The *brāhmaṇa* opened his eyes and cried out, "Oh, my!" Jagannātha Miśra came and saw what had happened. He was furious and ran behind Nimāī while verbally chastising Him and trying to catch Him. Nimāī was scared and fled away into a bedroom. Viśvarūpa entered at that moment. Seeing His effulgent form, the *brāhmaṇa* became very pleased and asked who he was. Viśvarūpa replied that he was the son of Jagannātha Miśra. Viśvarūpa offered his obeisance and requested the *brāhmaṇa* to kindly cook one more time for his deity. The *brāhmaṇa* again expressed how he felt it was the desire of the Lord that he just eat fruits and roots today, which was the norm for him as he was a wandering mendicant. Viśvarūpa fell at the *brāhmaṇa's* feet and begged him to cook once more as, if he fasted in their house, there would be inauspiciousness.

It was already nighttime, but the *brāhmaṇa* agreed to cook due to Viśvarūpa's wonderful qualities. This time, Jagannātha Miśra himself guarded the door of the Ṭhākura-ghara where the food would be offered to Bāla-gopāla. The *brāhmaṇa* cooked and brought the offering to his *śālagrāma* and sat down to meditate on feeding Bāla-gopāla through meditation. Out of divine will, everyone in the house fell asleep and Nimāī escaped out of His room and entered the room where the *brāhmaṇa* was offering the food. Immediately, he opened his eyes and cried, "Oh my! Oh my!" This time, Nimāī spoke: "O *brāhmaṇa*! You are so generous. You call Me, so what is My fault in coming? You meditate on My mantra and summon Me. I can't stay away when you call Me, so I come wherever you call Me. You always think of seeing Me and thus I have given you a vision of Myself."

At that instant, Nimāī manifested the divine Vṛndāvana-dhāma with a *kadamba* tree, cows, cowherd boys, cowherd girls, and singing birds surrounding Himself; Nimāī had taken on the form of Kṛṣṇa with eight hands. Four hands were holding the conch shell, discus (*cakra*), club, and lotus. One hand was holding butter and the other hand was taking the butter to eat it. The last two hands were holding the flute. He had a beautiful flower garland swinging on His neck from here to there. His lips were reddish, and He had lotus-petal-shaped eyes. His face was like a full moon and His ears were adorned with shark-shaped earrings. His chest was adorned with the mark of Śrīvatsa and the Kaustubha jewel. His whole body was decorated with jewels. He had a peacock feather on His head and was wearing a *guñjā* necklace. His divine feet were adorned with anklets and His jewel-like nails drove the darkness of the night far away. This form of Kṛṣṇa was what the *brāhmaṇa* meditated on daily. Seeing this same form before his very eyes, he fainted out of bliss. Kṛṣṇa touched him and he regained consciousness.

The *brāhmaṇa* was speechless and repeatedly fell on the floor, offering his obeisance. Out of ecstasy, he was trembling and sweating, and his hairs stood on end. Tears were flowing from his eyes like the Gaṅgā. He held onto Kṛṣṇa's divine feet and began to cry loudly. Gaurasundara told the *brāhmaṇa* that he had been His devotee in Dvāpara-yuga, and the same pastime had occurred in Nanda Mahārāja's home at Gokula, and that He had eaten the *brāhmaṇa's* food in Gokula as well. Gaurasundara said, "I have appeared in this form to spread the congregational chanting of the Hare Kṛṣṇa *mahā-mantra* and to freely distribute the divine love (*prema-bhakti*), which is desired by even Lord Brahmā." Nimāī went back to His room and went back to sleep as if nothing had happened. The *brāhmaṇa* was dancing, singing, and laughing in ecstasy; he was rubbing the rice all over his body and was repeatedly saying, "Jaya Bāla-gopāla!" When the family members woke up, the *brāhmaṇa* thought to tell everyone about their son being the Supreme Lord but remembered that Nimāī had forbade him to tell anyone. From then onwards, the *brāhmaṇa* lived near the Lord and came to see Him every day under the pretext of begging for alms. Such are the glories of Gaurasundara, which even the Vedas are unaware of.

Nimāī's First Words

On an auspicious day and time, Jagannātha Miśra performed the ceremony of having Nimāī write His first words, marking the beginning of His education. On the same day, Nimāī's ears were pierced, and His head was shaved. The inner meaning of piercing the ears is for the child to begin studying spiritual matters and take away all focus from topics that are inferior to Kṛṣṇa. Nimāī could easily write down all the letters and everyone was totally surprised at how such a young child could write so well. Within two to three days, he was writing combined consonants and syllables. Then, He was writing different names of the Lord, such as "Rāma, Kṛṣṇa, Mukunda, Murāri, Vanamālī," and so on. Nimāī would pronounce the vowels and syllables very sweetly.

Everyone would forget themselves watching the wonders of the child Nimāī. Nimāī would tell people to get him the birds that were flying in the sky. Sometimes He would ask people to get the moon and stars from the sky. When they would express that they were unable to get those things for Him, Nimāī would start rolling on the ground crying. Only when they chanted the holy names would He stop crying. This was one of Nimāī's strategies to get all the townspeople to chant the holy names of Hari.

A Teaching from Mother Śacī

One day, Śacī Mātā gave Nimāī some sweetmeats (*sandeśa*) and went to do her household work. Instead of eating the *sandeśa*, Nimāī began eating mud. When Śacī Mātā saw this, she threw the mud out of Nimāī's mouth and asked Him why He was eating the mud instead of the *sandeśa*. Nimāī said, "Mother, what's My fault? You gave Me mud to eat. *Sandeśa* is mud; if you leave the *sandeśa* on the mud, after some days, it will just turn into mud. Then again, *sandeśa* is made from mud. This is because grass grows from mud. Cows eat the grass and produce milk. That milk is made into cottage cheese (*chaanaa*, which is soft *paneer*). Also, sugar comes from sugar cane, which also comes from the mud. *Sandeśa* is made by combining *chaanaa* with sugar. Therefore, isn't *sandeśa* just a transformation of mud? Thus, eating *sandeśa* and eating mud is one and the same."

Hearing her son's words, Śacī Mātā was amazed and said, "Who gave You the knowledge that You should eat mud? If You eat the transformation of mud, which becomes rice, then Your body gets nourished. If You eat just mud, then You get diseased, and Your body gets destroyed. When mud is transformed into a clay pot, then it can be filled with water. The mud becomes a lump when it sucks up water." Then, Nimāī hid His true identity and asked, "Mother, why didn't you teach Me this before? Now I understand

and I will not eat mud. When I feel hungry, then I will drink milk from your breast." Those who think that Nimāī is just made of the illusory energy and who do not understand His true divine nature will only have the knowledge to eat mud; they will not understand the true knowledge.

Ekādaśī Pastimes

Nimāī would stop crying immediately upon hearing the singing of the holy names. However, one day, it was Ekādaśī, and Nimāī just wouldn't stop crying. When His mother asked what would make Him stop crying, Nimāī said, "If I can eat the many offerings that Hiraṇya and Jagadīśa have made, then I will be happy." Everyone was so surprised to hear Nimāī's words as the house of Hiraṇya and Jagadīśa was about three kilometers to the south. Hiraṇya and Jagadīśa were unalloyed devotees of Viṣṇu. They used to fast on Ekādaśī but would prepare many delicious offerings for Lord Viṣṇu. But how did Nimāī know about it? Everyone was amazed at this point.

Jagannātha Miśra went to their house and told them about what Nimāī had said. Hiraṇya and Jagadīśa were great devotees and immediately understood that Nimāī was not an ordinary child. They said, "We have understood that this boy is most beautiful. Thus, Gopāla Himself must be present in this boy. Nārāyaṇa plays through this boy; sitting in the boy's heart, He speaks." They immediately took all the offerings that they had prepared and went with Jagannātha Miśra to offer everything to Nimāī. Everyone was in great bliss. *Caitanya-bhāgavata* states: "The Lord happily eats the offerings of His devotees. And Nimāī's intense hunger was appeased. Everyone happily chanted, 'Hari! Hari!' Nimāī would sometimes throw the food on the floor and sometimes on someone's body. Like this, the controller of the past, present, and future displayed His pastimes. The master who is described in all the Vedas is playing in such a manner in the courtyard of Śacī Mātā". (*Ādi-khaṇḍa* 6.38-41)

Another time, Nimāī told His mother that He wanted her to give Him a donation. Śacī Mātā said, "I will give You whatever You want." Then, Nimāī said, "You shall not eat rice on Ekādaśī." Śacī Mātā agreed and from that day onward, she did not eat grains on Ekādaśī. In this way, Nimāī was teaching everyone that they should not eat grains on the day of Ekādaśī, as it is a day that is most dear to Lord Hari. According to that tradition, we do not take any grains on Ekādaśī.

Nimāī's Mischievous Activities

Nimāī was very mischievous. When people would be taking bath in the Gaṅgā, Nimāī would splash water on everyone and play in the water. Through His play, the divine water that washed Nimāī's feet would be splashed on everyone. Even though everyone tried to stop His mischief, He refused to stay in one place. Sometimes a person would be coming out of the Gaṅgā after finishing his bath and Nimāī would intentionally throw sand on that person so that that person would have to bathe again. Other times, while someone was taking bath in the Gaṅgā, Nimāī would take water in His mouth and spit it out on the person. People complained to Jagannātha Miśra, saying that they could not properly meditate while bathing in the Gaṅgā due to Nimāī's mischief. They would complain to Jagannātha Miśra, telling him that Nimāī says to them that He, Himself, is the Supreme Lord Nārāyaṇa. Some people would complain that Nimāī took away their Śiva *liṅga* and others would complain about how Nimāī took away their clothes, *pūjā* offerings, and paraphernalia and would flee away. Nimāī would say, "The person whom you are worshiping is personally taking the offerings. That person is Me, so why are you complaining?" Some people would be chanting their *gāyatrī* mantras, standing waste deep in the Gaṅgā, and Nimāī would go and pull their legs.

The men of Navadvīpa would complain to Jagannātha Miśra. The young girls would become angry and complain to Śacī Mātā about Nimāī. They complained about how Nimāī would steal their clothing while they bathed in the Gaṅgā, and if they said anything to Him, then He would throw water on them. Nimāī would take away all their offerings which they had brought for worship. He would also throw sand on them and spit water at the girls. Sometimes, He would throw the seeds of *okara* fruit, which would get stuck in their hair. Nimāī would say that He wanted to marry some of them and sometimes He would go and yell loudly in their ears when they were unaware that He was present. The women used to say how they heard that Nanda Mahārāja's son would do mischief and that Nimāī was behaving in the same way. Śacī Mātā would say, "I will punish Him, and He will not do all this again in the future." In fact, everyone was secretly happy due to Nimāī's mischief, but they would externally complain. Nimāī would act like He had never committed any of the mischief that people complained about.

Viśvarūpa Leaves Home

Viśvarūpa was the elder brother of Nimāī. The only person in front of whom Nimāī would stop His mischievous behavior was Viśvarūpa. Viśvarūpa was renounced from birth and was anointed with all good qualities. He always showed how devotion to Kṛṣṇa was the purport of all scriptures. In this way, Viśvarūpa engaged all his senses in the service of Kṛṣṇa. Although he knew that his younger brother was Bāla-gopāla, he did not reveal that secret to anybody. Viśvarūpa was always absorbed in listening to topics about Kṛṣṇa and performing various services for Kṛṣṇa.

All the materialistic people of the time were proud, and they all had the seed of hate towards Viṣṇu and the Vaiṣṇavas. Even those who claimed to be teachers of the *Bhagavad-gītā* and *Śrīmad-Bhāgavatam* had no tinge of devotion to Kṛṣṇa within them. Thus, seeing the suffering of all these living entities, Advaita Ācārya and the pure devotees used to cry. Similarly, Viśvarūpa decided not to look at the faces of the worldly people and to renounce the world. Every morning, Viśvarūpa would take a bath in the Gaṅgā and go to Advaita Ācārya's home to listen to his descriptions of how devotion to Kṛṣṇa is the essence of all scriptures. Śacī Devī would send Nimāī every day to bring His elder brother home for lunch from Advaita Ācārya's class. Viśvarūpa would go home just for name's sake and then would immediately go back to Advaita Ācārya's home. Even when he came home, Viśvarūpa would never get involved in any household affairs and would always stay in the temple room of Lord Viṣṇu.

When Viśvarūpa heard that his parents were planning to get him married, he became extremely sad. Within a few days, left home and took up the vow of renunciation (*sannyāsa*). He then became known as Śrī Śaṅkarāraṇya. Śacī Mātā and Jagannātha Miśra felt much pain in their hearts and Gaurasundara performed the pastime of fainting out of separation from His elder brother. Advaita Ācārya and the other devotees cried out of feeling the pain of separation from Viśvarūpa. All the friends came to give some consolation to Śacī Mātā and Jagannātha Miśra. When the devotees heard of Viśvarūpa's *sannyāsa*, they wanted to all leave for the forest out of feeling so much sadness in their hearts. Advaita Ācārya explained to everyone that Kṛṣṇa would soon appear in their hearts, take away all their sadness, and that the Lord would reciprocate with them.

Nimāī's Thirst for Education

After Viśvarūpa's departure, Nimāī began focusing on His studies and always stayed by the side of His parents. Śacī Mātā was blissful upon hearing about the extraordinary intelligence of her son. However, Jagannātha Miśra became afraid that Nimāī would also realize the temporary nature of the material world and the essence of devotion to Kṛṣṇa, and that he would then follow in the footsteps of His elder brother. After discussing with Śacī Mātā, Jagannātha Miśra decided to put a stop to Nimāī's education. In response to this, Nimāī used His precocious intelligence to force His parents to send Him to school. One day, Śacī Mātā scolded Nimāī for some childish misdemeanor, and the boy went off in a huff to sit on a pile of refuse. When she started to chastise Him for getting dirty, Nimāī cleverly answered, "You won't let Me go to school. I am supposed to be a *brāhmaṇa*, but if I am not educated, how will I be able to distinguish good from bad? I am illiterate, so how can you expect Me to tell the difference between a pure place and an impure one? It's all the same to Me." (*Caitanya-bhāgavata, Ādi-khaṇḍa* 7.269-270)

After hearing Nimāī speak in this way, Jagannātha Miśra decided it was pointless to hold Him back and so enrolled him in the school of Gaṇgādāsa Paṇḍita. In a very short time, Nimāī had mastered Sanskrit grammar and much more. If He encountered any scholar on the street, the proud boy would challenge him with trick questions about grammar or logic. The town's *paṇḍitas* would be embarrassed by their inability to answer Nimāī and so would immediately cross the street to avoid Him. However, by His behavior, Nimāī was teaching the real purpose of learning through His actions:

paḍe kene loka kṛṣṇa-bhakti jānibāre
se yadi nahila tabe vidyāya ki kare
(*Caitanya-bhāgavata, Ādi-khaṇḍa* 12.49)

> "What is the purpose of learning? It's to know about devotion to Kṛṣṇa. If one does not learn this, then what is the point of being educated?"

Jagannātha Miśra left this world before Nimāī had finished His schooling. Nimāī dutifully performed the customary funeral rites for His father and then returned to concentrating on His studies. Before long, His reputation as a brilliant student had spread far and wide and He was able to open a small school and take students of His own.

Nimāī Enters Married Life

Not long afterward, Nimāī was married to Lākṣmī Priya Devī, the daughter of Vallabha Ācārya. A few months after the wedding, He set off for East Bengal, or what is now Bangladesh, on a teaching tour to earn some money. His reputation was greatly enhanced on this trip, but when He returned, He found that Lākṣmī Priya Devī had been bitten by a snake during His absence and was no longer in this world. Seeing how grief-stricken His mother was, Nimāī spoke the following words to console her:

> "O Mother! Why are you so sad? How can anyone fight their destiny? In the passage of time, no person belongs to anyone else. That is why the Vedas always emphasize that this world is temporary. The whole creation is governed by the will of God. Who else but He brings us together or separates us from each other? If everything happens according to the will of God, then nothing should cause us distress! Furthermore, it is considered a sign of good fortune for a woman to die before her husband rather than being left a widow herself. Is Lakṣmī not most fortunate?" (*Caitanya-bhāgavata, Ādi-khaṇḍa* 14.183-187)

For the next year, Nimāī taught at the house of Mukunda Sañjaya. He would tutor His students from early morning until noon, and then pursue His own studies through the afternoon until late at night. In the meantime, Śacī Devī became anxious to see her son married again. She engaged Kāśinātha Paṇḍita to broker Nimāī's marriage to Viṣṇupriyā, the saintly daughter of Sanātana Miśra. Sanātana Miśra was a *brāhmaṇa* from a respected family, a great devotee of Viṣṇu who possessed many good qualities: he was charitable, a welcoming host, truthful, and self-controlled. Furthermore, as a scholar to the royal court, he was very wealthy. Another wealthy citizen of the town, Buddhimanta Khān, volunteered to finance the wedding. In Satya-yuga, Buddhimanta Khān was Suvarṇa Sena. When the auspicious moment came, Nimāī set off with great pomp in a festive wedding procession to Sanātana Miśra's house. The rituals were carried out, and the couple was united in marriage.

Loving Quarrels with Śrīdhara

One day, Nimāī went to the house of Śrīdhara, who was a poor salesman of banana stem, leaves, and fruits. Nimāī loved Śrīdhara and used to go to his house on various occasions. He would joke with Śrīdhara and discuss various topics for about forty-five minutes to an hour and a half when He would visit. Nimāī asked Śrīdhara, "You always say, 'Hari! Hari!' Then, why do you suffer? You don't have enough food or proper clothing." Śrīdhara replied, "It's not that I fast. Whether there is expensive or cheap clothing, I do have clothes to wear." Nimāī explained that Śrīdhara's clothes had about ten knots, showing that his clothes were so old that there were so many holes in them, and those holes had to be tied up. Nimāī said, "I see that there is not even a proper straw roof on your house. These materialistic worshipers of Caṇḍī Devī have nice homes, food, and clothes."

Śrīdhara replied, "O *brāhmaṇa*! You've spoken great words. However, time passes for everyone in the same manner. The king stays in a bejeweled palace, eats opulent foods, and wears fancy clothes. The birds live on the trees, yet time passes the same for all. Everybody enjoys the fruits of their actions according to the desire of the Lord." Nimāī said, "You have so much wealth, but you are hiding it and eating. I will make that wealth known in some days. Then I will see how you will try to deceive the people." Śrīdhara said, "Please go home, O scholar! It is not proper for You and I to argue." Nimāī then replied, "I will not leave you just like that! What will you give Me? Tell Me right this moment." Śrīdhara explained, "I sell the outer layers of the banana tree trunks and eat and maintain myself in this way. What will I give You from this, tell me, Gosāī?" Nimāī stated, "Let your real treasure stay with you for now. I will take that later. For now, just give Me bananas, radishes, and banana stems for free. If you give them to Me, then I will not argue with you." Śrīdhara thought in his mind, "This *brāhmaṇa* is so aggressive. If I don't follow His instructions, then He may even beat me up. Even if He hits me, what can I do to the *brāhmaṇa*? I don't have the ability to give anything for free every day. However, whatever the *brāhmaṇa* takes is certainly my own fortune. I will give Him free vegetables every day."

Brāhmaṇas are to be respected in society. Thus, Śrīdhara was thinking that even if the *brāhmaṇa* Nimāī hit him, he would not do anything to retaliate. Rather, whatever help can be given to the *brāhmaṇas* is an opportunity to gain unknown spiritual credits known as *ajñāta-sukṛti*. Then Śrīdhara said to Nimāī, "Listen, Gosāī! You will not be responsible to pay for anything. I will give You whatever You want, including banana stems, bananas, and radishes for free. Don't argue with me anymore." Nimāī said, "Good, good! No more arguments. Make sure I get good quality banana stems and bananas." Nimāī constantly ate His meals on the outer coverings of the trunks of the banana trees, which were previously used as plates. He would get these from Śrīdhara. In addition to the bananas, radishes, and banana stems, Nimāī would also eat the bottle gourds that He got from Śrīdhara. The bottle gourds would be cooked with milk and pepper.

Nimāī said, "What do you think of Me, Śrīdhara? You think I will go home just like this?" Śrīdhara said, "You are a *brāhmaṇa*—a part of Viṣṇu." Nimāī said, "You don't know that I'm actually a cowherd boy. You see Me as a son of a *brāhmaṇa*. But I am a cowherd boy." Śrīdhara laughed hearing Nimāī's words. He couldn't understand His own Lord due to the power of Māyā Devī (illusion). Nimāī said, "Śrīdhara, I will tell you the truth. Your Gaṅgā's glories originate from Me." Śrīdhara said, "O Paṇḍita Nimāī! You are not afraid of speaking about the Gaṅgā in such a way? Usually, people become less mischievous as they grow older, but it seems that Your mischief has doubled with age." In this way, Nimāī had such loving pastimes with Śrīdhara and then went home.

Defeating the Scholar Who Had Conquered All Directions

At about this time, Keśava Kāśmīrī, a famous scholar who made his living by traveling and engaging other scholars in debate, arrived in Navadvīpa.

Navadvīpa's *paṇḍitas* were afraid of being defeated by the Kāśmīrī *brāhmaṇa* and losing their own reputations, as well as losing the town's reputation as a center of learning. They consulted among themselves and decided to appoint Nimāī as their representative. Their reasoning was that if the young scholar lost, no real harm would be done to Navadvīpa's reputation. On the other hand, if He won, it would be a feather in everyone's cap. Were Keśava Kāśmīrī to be defeated by a mere boy, he would depart in shame and not bother to challenge any of the town's other scholars.

One night, Mahāprabhu was seated with His students on the bank of the Ganges, teaching them Sanskrit grammar. Keśava Kāśmīrī offered obeisance to mother Gaṅgā and then went to meet Nimāī Paṇḍita. After Mahāprabhu had Keśava Kāśmīrī seated with respect, Keśava Kāśmīrī began to speak in a mood of neglect. He said, "Nimāī, You teach Sanskrit grammar and that's why You are known as a scholar. You teach a scripture which is for little children and everyone glorifies You. I have heard that You answer Your students' complicated questions while You teach the Kalāpa Sanskrit grammar." Nimāī replied, "I am so proud because I teach Sanskrit grammar. My students don't even understand, and I am not able to make them understand. You are an expert in all scriptures. Where am I? I am just a new child. I want to hear some of your poetry. If you have mercy, please describe the glories of the Gaṅgā."

The *brāhmaṇa* Keśava Kāśmīrī began to proudly glorify the Ganges at the speed of the wind; he composed one hundred verses in one hour. Nimāī Paṇḍita glorified Keśava Kāśmīrī's poetic skills and said that he must be the recipient of Sarasvatī Devī's mercy. He then asked Keśava Kāśmīrī to explain a specific verse and when the scholar asked which verse, Nimāī Paṇḍita replied saying:

mahattvaṁ gaṅgāyāḥ satatam idam ābhāti nitarāṁ
yad eṣā śrī-viṣṇoś caraṇa-kamalotpatti-subhagā
dvitīya-śrī-lakṣmīr iva sura-narair arcya-caraṇā
bhavānī-bhartur yā śirasi vibhavaty adbhuta-guṇā

(*Caitanya-caritāmṛta, Ādi-līlā* 16.41)

"Gaṅgā Devī's glories are effulgent as she is most fortunate. She originates from the lotus feet of Lord Viṣṇu and she is like a second Lakṣmī Devī.

> She is worshiped by the gods and humans. She has amazing qualities and even has influence over the husband of Bhavānī Devī."

Keśava Kāśmīrī was astounded. He said, "I spoke as fast as the wind blows during a storm. How did You choose this verse out of all those verses that I composed?" Mahāprabhu replied, "By whose mercy you have conquered all directions, can someone not gain the ability to remember everything he hears from that same person from whom you got the special mercy?" As soon as Nimāī Paṇḍita explained the five faults of this verse, Keśava Kāśmīrī became extremely angry. Nimāī Paṇḍita explained, in detail, the Sanskrit grammatical mistakes Keśava Kāśmīrī had made and said, "Even though there may be ten beautiful ornamentations in a verse, one fault destroys all of the ornamentations. Herein, there were five faults!"

Keśava Kāśmīrī accepted defeat and his face became pale. Nimāī Paṇḍita offered respects to him and said, "It is very late in the night. Take some rest. Come tomorrow. We can discuss." Keśava Kāśmīrī began thinking, "Maybe I have made some offense at the divine feet of Sarasvatī Devī." He did not eat and began chanting his mantra, thus meditating on Sarasvatī Devī. Sarasvatī Devī appeared to him and said, "You were victorious all this time and had elephants, horses, fame, and so on. That is not my true mercy. Today, you received my true mercy. Śrī Nimāī Paṇḍita is the Supreme Lord; He is my eternal Lord. You are most fortunate to have been defeated by Him. Now become blessed by surrendering unto His divine lotus feet. I am the servant of His divine lotus feet. I stay behind Him out of shyness." Keśava Kāśmīrī therefore received true knowledge by the mercy of Sarasvatī Devī.

The next morning, Nimāī Paṇḍita was sitting with His students. Keśava Kāśmīrī offered his prostrate obeisance. Mahāprabhu said, "Oh! What are you doing? You are such a big scholar; why are you behaving in such a way?" Keśava Kāśmīrī replied, "Sarasvatī Devī told me about Your true identity. Master, have mercy on me. I have taken shelter at Your divine lotus feet." Nimāī Paṇḍita embraced Keśava Kāśmīrī and explained the concepts of establishing a relationship with the Supreme Lord (*sambandha*), how to act upon that relationship (*abhidheya*), and how to attain the ultimate goal (*prayojana*). Keśava Kāśmīrī expressed his repentance and then his heart became illuminated with knowledge, renunciation, and devotion. True knowledge is to engage in service and remembrance of the Supreme Lord. In this way, Keśava Kāśmīrī's life became perfected by obtaining the divine lotus feet of Mahāprabhu through the strength of knowledge. After this incident, Keśava Kāśmīrī decided to take the renounced order and became an Ācārya in the line of Nimbārka Ācārya.

Part II
The Transformation

Nimāī's Transformation

Despite being wed to a beautiful and virtuous wife, Nimāī's interest in married life slowly waned. In early 1509, when He was nearly twenty-three years old, He traveled to Gayā to offer oblations at the holy Brahma-kuṇḍa for the repose of His departed father's soul. After He had bathed in Brahma-kuṇḍa and finished these sacred rites, Nimāī went to Chakrabera Tīrtha, where the famous temple of Lord Viṣṇu's lotus feet stands. While meditating there, He heard someone reciting the glories of the Deity from the scriptures. He began to experience transcendental ecstatic symptoms, and a veritable Ganges of tears flowed from His eyes.

While still in this condition, Nimāī met Īśvara Purī, who was to become His spiritual master. As soon as they saw each other, they were both overwhelmed by waves of ecstatic love for Kṛṣṇa. Nimāī told Īśvara Purī that His actual purpose in coming to Gayā had been to meet him:

> My trip to Gayā became a success as soon as I saw your lotus feet. One who comes here to offer oblations delivers his forefathers and perhaps himself as well. As soon as I saw you, however, millions of forefathers were immediately delivered from their material bondage. No holy place could ever be your equal. Indeed, saints like you are the only real reason any holy place is able to sanctify the pilgrim. Please

> lift Me out of this ocean of material entanglement. I hereby surrender My body and life to you. All I ask of you is that you please give Me the nectar of Kṛṣṇa's lotus feet to drink.
>
> (*Caitanya-bhāgavata, Ādi-khaṇḍa* 17.50-55)

Chaitanya Mahāprabhu thus emphasized that the greatest benefit that comes from visiting places of pilgrimage is meeting the holy people who frequent them. Therefore, no one should think that visiting a place of pilgrimage is ever equal to coming in contact with an authentic saint or spiritual master. The spiritual master is so powerful that he can bestow upon us a taste for the nectar of service to Kṛṣṇa, which is the highest purpose in life according to Mahāprabhu. The truth is that Chaitanya Mahāprabhu is the universal spiritual master; He is Kṛṣṇa, incarnating as His own devotee in the mood of Rādhārāṇī to distribute the means for attaining love of God. Nevertheless, to teach the necessity of taking initiation from a bona fide spiritual master, He displayed this pastime of receiving the ten-syllable Kṛṣṇa mantra from Īśvara Purī.

After initiation, Nimāī became permanently intoxicated with devotion to Kṛṣṇa. On His return home to Navadvīpa, He was no longer the same proud but fun-loving scholar He had been. He was completely indifferent to all His previous preoccupations, including family life. He stopped teaching His students and even closed His school. He spent all his time looking everywhere for Kṛṣṇa, calling out Kṛṣṇa's name, and fainting due to separation from Kṛṣṇa.

Soon thereafter, Nimāī began to participate in *kīrtanas*, or ecstatic festivals of singing and dancing to the holy names of Kṛṣṇa, in the house of Śrīvasa Paṇḍita, an elderly Vaiṣṇava who lived nearby. To this day, Śrīvāsa's house is called the "Saṅkīrtana Rāsa Sthali," in reference to the place where Kṛṣṇa had His *rāsa* dance with the *gopīs*. Just as that was the most significant of Kṛṣṇa's pastimes, *saṅkīrtana* is the most significant of Mahāprabhu's pastimes. Mahāprabhu also held *kīrtanas* from time to time in the house of Candraśekhara Ācārya.

The vibrations of this *kīrtana* washed over the land as far as Śāntipura. Soon thereafter, all of Mahāprabhu's associates—Nityānanda Prabhu, Advaita Prabhu, Haridāsa Ṭhākura, Gadādhara Paṇḍita, Śrīvāsa Paṇḍita, Puṇḍarīka

Vidyānidhi, Murāri Gupta, Hiraṇya, Gaṅgādāsa, Vanamālī, Vijaya, Nandana Ācārya, Jagadānanda, Buddhimanta Khān, Nārāyaṇa Paṇḍita, Kāśīśvara, Vāsudeva, Śrī Rāma Paṇḍita, Śrī Govinda, Govindānanda, Gopīnātha, Jagadīśa, Śrīdhara Paṇḍita, and many others—came to join Him in the nightly chanting. This was the beginning of the *saṅkīrtana* movement. It was as though the transcendental God of love had descended from the spiritual sky, conquering over the hearts of everyone and manifesting on their tongues in the form of Kṛṣṇa's sweet name.

Cāpāla Gopāla Offends Śrīvāsa Paṇḍita

The people of Navadvīpa were all getting very much attracted to Mahāprabhu's *saṅkīrtana* in Śrīvāsa's house, which would occur behind closed doors throughout the night. People who were not pure devotees of Kṛṣṇa were not allowed to enter the *kīrtanas* going on in Śrīvāsa's home. Many people born in *brāhmaṇa* families wanted to make fun of the *saṅkīrtana* going on inside Śrīvāsa's house. The common people who were usually attached to these *brāhmaṇas* were now becoming attracted towards the *saṅkīrtana* movement. Therefore, one night, out of jealousy, a Bhaṭṭācārya *brāhmaṇa* known as Cāpāla Gopāla placed all the ingredients needed for performing Bhavānī Devī's *pūjā* outside the door of Śrīvāsa's home. These ingredients included banana leaves, turmeric root, hibiscus flowers, vermilion, red sandalwood, and rice grains. In addition, he placed a pot of wine. The next morning when Śrīvāsa Paṇḍita opened the door of his house, he saw all the ingredients. Due to extreme purity and devotion to Kṛṣṇa, he was totally calm. Rather than reacting with negativity, Śrīvāsa Paṇḍita called all his neighbors and declared, "See! I perform worship of Bhavānī Devī every night. I am a worshiper of *śakti*." However, none of the gentlemen believed Śrīvāsa Paṇḍita; rather, they knew that some wicked person had placed all those ingredients in front of the door to taint Śrīvāsa Paṇḍita's reputation. They called a cleaner to remove all the ingredients and had the floor cleaned with cow dung.

Within three days, Cāpāla Gopāla's body was afflicted with leprosy and blood was oozing from everywhere; insects were crawling in all the sores of rotten flesh. He suffered unbearable pain. One day, Cāpāla Gopāla went in front of Mahāprabhu and, crying, offered his obeisance. He said, "You have come here to deliver the residents of this world. You are full of mercy and You feel great pain when You see others suffering. Thus, I have come to You. I am dying from the burning sensation caused by this leprosy. Tell me the way to be free from this disease." Mahāprabhu said, "Go far away! Go far away! O sinful one, if people see you, they accumulate sins. Even if a greatly religious person sees you, then he must suffer on that day. You are most fallen and sinful as you are a criticizer of Vaiṣṇavas. You have much more suffering to endure. You are not able to suffer this burning sensation, so how will you tolerate the suffering that is waiting for you in hell? The whole world becomes purified by hearing the name of the Vaiṣṇavas. Brahmā sings about the glories of the characters of the Vaiṣṇavas. By serving the Vaiṣṇavas, one can attain the inconceivable Kṛṣṇa. There is no worship higher than worship of the Vaiṣṇavas. The *Śrīmad-Bhāgavatam* says that the Vaiṣṇavas are dearer to Kṛṣṇa than even Ananta Śeṣa, Lakṣmī, Brahma, and Śiva. One who criticizes the Vaiṣṇavas will suffer during his lifetime and even after death. Such a sinful and fallen person's education, familial lineage, and austerities are all fruitless. Kṛṣṇa doesn't even accept worship from such a person. The world becomes blessed from the dancing of the Vaiṣṇavas. The ten directions become purified of their sins when the Vaiṣṇavas look their way. When the Vaiṣṇavas dance while raising their arms, even the obstacles in heaven are destroyed. Śrīvāsa Paṇḍita is such an exalted devotee and you, sinful one, criticized his character. What to speak of your suffering from leprosy? Your real punishment is waiting to be given by Dharma-rāja. You are not worthy to be seen by Me. I cannot cure you of your suffering." Thereafter, Mahāprabu bathed in the Gaṅgā and left.

In the future, after Mahāprabhu had taken *sannyāsa* and came to Kuliyā village in Bengal from Jagannātha Purī, Cāpāla Gopāla approached Him again, having understood his own mistake. He begged Mahāprabhu for a solution to his problems, which were due to him committing offenses to Śrīvāsa out of pride. Mahāprabhu said that the only way to be forgiven was to beg for forgiveness at Śrīvāsa Paṇḍita's divine lotus feet. Mahāprabhu explained that one must beg for forgiveness from the person at whose feet he committed an offense; just like if a thorn goes into one's foot, that thorn must be removed by using another thorn. Mahāprabhu said, "If Śrīvāsa forgives you, then you will be free from suffering. He is of extremely pure intelligence. He will forgive you and deliver you, easily." In this way, Cāpāla Gopāla begged for forgiveness from Śrīvāsa Paṇḍita and was ultimately forgiven for the offense committed out of great pride; thus, he became free from his leprosy.

The Meeting of Nityānanda and Chaitanya

Nityānanda Prabhu was the son of Hāḍāi Ojhā and Padmāvatī Devī. He was born in Rāḍhadeśa and used to worship Lord Śiva there named Mauḍeśvara. His parents loved Him very much and could not stay for even a fraction of a second away from Him. One day, a traveling *sannyāsī* came to Rādhadeśa and was served by Hāḍāi Paṇḍita and his wife very nicely. When the traveling *sannyāsī* was leaving, he requested Hāḍāi Paṇḍita to give him Nityānanda Prabhu as his traveling *brāhmaṇa* assistant, as he would be traveling to various holy places. Despite feeling great reluctance and grief, Hāḍāi Paṇḍita and Padmāvatī Devī agreed to hand over their son. In this way, Nityānanda Prabhu left home along with the traveling *sannyāsī*. Actually, Nityānanda Prabhu had the desire to leave home earlier, and in this manner, He was relieved from family life.

After traveling all over the length and breadth of India, Nityānanda Prabhu went to Vṛndāvana and waited there until the right time to go to Navadvīpa to meet Mahāprabhu. In Vṛndāvana, Nityānanda Prabhu was always in a child-like mood and was constantly chanting the names of Kṛṣṇa. He never cared to eat. Mahāprabhu was feeling sad in Navadvīpa and wanted to meet Nityānanda Prabhu as well. One day, Nityānanda suddenly arrived in Navadvīpa and began to stay at the house of Nandana Ācārya. Mahāprabhu knew that He had come and indicated this information to His associates. Mahāprabhu explained that He had a dream in which a great, divine personality came in a chariot with a palm-tree on its flag and asked ten to twenty times, "Is this the house of Nimāī Paṇḍita?" In this way, Mahāprabhu sent out His associates to look for this personality, but they could not find Him anywhere. Finally, Mahāprabhu decided to personally go out and look for this great personality. Mahāprabhu, along with His associates, arrived at the house of Nandana Ācārya. There, they saw a divine, effulgent personality sitting in deep meditation. They all offered their obeisance. Mahāprabhu indicated to Śrīvasa Paṇḍita to recite a verse from the *Śrīmad-Bhāgavatam*. Śrīvasa Paṇḍita then recited the verse explaining the beauty of Kṛṣṇa as He enters the forest of Vṛndāvana. Hearing that verse, Nityānanda Prabhu immediately fainted. After some time, He regained consciousness, and when He heard the verse again, Nityānanda Prabhu again fell to the ground. Various symptoms of divine ecstasy were manifest on His body. He then lay down on the lap of Nimāī. Gadādhara Paṇḍita understood how the opposite of normalcy was taking place: Ananta Śeṣa Himself was lying on the lap of the Mahā-Viṣṇu. Then, Gaurasundara began glorifying Nitāī and expressing the mysteries of His existence. Nitāī, in turn, explained how Mahāprabhu was Kṛṣṇa Himself. Nityānanda and Mahāprabhu were communicating in such a way that only the two of them could understand each other; nobody else could understand. In this way, the transcendental meeting of Nitāī and Chaitanya took place in Nandana Ācārya's house in the presence of all the intimate devotees.

The Hidden Nature of Puṇḍarīka Vidyānidhi

One day, Mahāprabhu suddenly got up and exclaimed, "Puṇḍarīka, My father!" and began crying. None of the surrounding devotees knew who Puṇḍarīka was. Subsequently, they asked Mahāprabhu about Puṇḍarīka. Mahāprabhu explained how externally, Puṇḍarīka Vidyānidhi looked like a materialist, but in reality, he was a *brāhmaṇa* who was totally devoted to God and who was totally uninvolved with materialist people. He was born in Chittagong, Bangladesh. He would always float in the ocean of devotion to Kṛṣṇa and his body was always anointed with tears, trembling, and hairs standing on end. He would not bathe in the Gaṅgā out of fear of his feet touching the water of the Gaṅgā. He would drink Gaṅgā water before engaging in worship. Mahāprabhu explained that he would soon be coming to Navadvīpa.

Shortly thereafter, Puṇḍarīka Vidyānidhi came to Navadvīpa with many servants, much wealth, *brāhmaṇas*, and disciples. He stayed in a hidden way in Navadvīpa and nobody could recognize who he really was. Only Mukunda Datta, who was born in Chittagong, knew of Puṇḍarīka Vidyānidhi's glories. One day, Mukunda told Gadādhara that he would take him to see a great devotee. When they reached the house of Puṇḍarīka Vidyānidhi, he spoke nicely with Gadādhara after hearing about him from Mukunda. However, seeing how Puṇḍarīka Vidyānidhi was living in such a royal way while chewing betel leaves, Gadādhara Paṇḍita felt some doubt in his mind. Understanding that Gadādhara Paṇḍita had a doubt, Mukunda began reciting the verse from the Śrī*mad-Bhāgavatam* about how Kṛṣṇa gave Pūtanā, the demoness who came to feed Him poison, a place equivalent to His wet nurse in the spiritual world. He gave her this position just because she had thought that Kṛṣṇa was such a beautiful baby and that she would like a baby like Him if she ever had one. Upon hearing this verse, Puṇḍarīka Vidyānidhi immediately went into a fit of ecstasy. He started crying and rolling on the ground. Seeing all these symptoms on his body, Gadādhara Paṇḍita realized that Puṇḍarīka Vidyānidhi was truly an extremely advanced devotee. Thereafter, Gadādhara Paṇḍita asked Mukunda to tell Puṇḍarīka Vidyānidhi that he wanted to take initiation from Puṇḍarīka Vidyānidhi and thereby nullify his offense of thinking doubtfully about this great devotee.

One night, Puṇḍarīka Vidyānidhi came to see Mahāprabhu, but out of divine ecstasy, he fainted and fell to the ground. After some time, he regained consciousness and began shouting different phrases while crying. Mahāprabhu recognized His dear devotee and embraced him while also crying. Mahāprabhu introduced Puṇḍarīka to all the devotees and glorified him. Thereafter, after coming back to normal consciousness, Puṇḍarīka Vidyānidhi offered his respects to all the devotees. Gadādhara Paṇḍita then asked for permission from Mahāprabhu to take initiation from Puṇḍarīka Vidyānidhi to be forgiven for his offense in the mind. Mahāprabhu blissfully gave him permission. Thereafter, Gadādhara Paṇḍita had the good fortune to receive initiation from Pundarika Vidyanidhi.

Devānanda Paṇḍita's Punishment

Devānanda Paṇḍita was a great scholar who was celibate from birth, desirous of liberation, and a great teacher of the Śrīmad-*Bhāgavatam*. However, he did not have devotion. One day, Śrīvāsa Paṇḍita went to the house of Devānanda Paṇḍita to hear his class on Śrīmad-*Bhāgavatam*. Knowing each of the letters of the Śrīmad-*Bhāgavatam* to be divine, Śrīvāsa

Paṇḍita went into ecstatic bliss and was crying. Seeing his transformations, the other students of Devānanda Paṇḍita thought Śrīvāsa Paṇḍita to be a disturbance to their studies. They therefore forcefully pulled him and took him out of the class. Śrīvāsa Paṇḍita went home feeling sad. When this happened, Devānanda Paṇḍita did not say anything to protest his students and thus accumulated the offense (*vaiṣṇava-aparādha*). Mahāprabhu went to see Devānanda Paṇḍita, and remembering this incident, He became very angry and scolded him. Devānanda Paṇḍita became shy and went back home. Ultimately, those who understand the punishment of Mahāprabhu to be a blessing also attain the greatest auspiciousness. In this manner, Mahāprabhu showed His intolerance of committing offense towards the Vaiṣṇavas.

Chand Kazi Threatens the Saṅkīrtana Movement

Atheists give the most importance to the physical body and the material world. Such atheists could not understand what was happening to Mahāprabhu after His transformation, any more than a barren woman can understand what it means to bear a child. Those whose only obsession is their day-to-day existence and who have no comprehension of love for God are called *pāṣaṇḍīs*. While the *pāṣaṇḍīs* of Navadvīpa had differing opinions about Mahāprabhu's *kīrtanas*, they were all against it. Some said that the devotees were disturbing the peace with their meaningless noise-making; others thought they were just drunkards partying. The *pāṣaṇḍīs* criticized and condemned, each according to their own misunderstanding, but the devotees paid them no attention. They simply remained absorbed in singing the holy names with Nimāī. When the *pāṣaṇḍīs* saw they were unable to put a stop to the *kīrtana* with their negative propaganda, they went to complain to the magistrate, or Kazi, who was the local representative of Bengal's Muslim ruler.

One day, while the Kazi was walking on the streets with his soldiers, he heard the sound of *mṛdaṅgas* coming from Śrīvāsa's house. Some Hindu *pāṣaṇḍīs* came and complained to the Kazi. Immediately, the Kazi, along with his soldiers, angrily entered Śrīvāsa's home and broke some *mṛdaṅgas* (clay drums used in *kīrtanas*). His eyes enraged, the Kazi said, "Today, I didn't give you all much of a punishment. In the future, if you don't follow my instructions and continue to sing *kīrtana* in loud voices, then I will force you to change your religion and take away all of your assets." Then the Kazi left, and all the devotees were shaking in fear. Śrī Gaurāṅga-deva, however, was burning in anger after hearing the events that took place that day.

The Kazi had ordered the *kīrtana* to be stopped, but Nimāī refused to obey such an unjust dictate. He proclaimed, "No one has the authority to stop the chanting of the holy names in this age of Kali." He ordered the devotees, "Go and perform *kīrtana*. Today I will put all the Muslims in their place! Light torches in every household. We'll see if the Kazi has the nerve to stop us!" (*Caitanya-caritāmṛta, Ādi-līlā* 17.130-134). He further declared, "Today we will hold *kīrtana* throughout Navadvīpa. We'll see who dares stop us. If we have to, we will burn down the Kazi's house and see what the king does about it. Today I will send down a great shower of love for Kṛṣṇa. The non-believers will meet their creator today!" (*Caitanya-bhāgavata, Madhya-khaṇḍa* 23.121-123).

Nimāī marshalled all the Vaiṣṇavas and their sympathizers into a huge protest march and fearlessly led the procession of chanters through the town up to the Kazi's house. There were hundreds of thousands of devotees. Once there, the agitated townspeople started to vandalize the house, flower gardens, and orchards. The few soldiers that the Kazi had were insignificant in number compared to the large numbers of townspeople who had taken Nimāī's side.

The Kazi was frightened by Nimāī's fearsome form and barricaded himself inside the house, keeping himself invisible. Nimāī became angry when the Kazi refused to meet with Him and said, "Where is that little rascal Kazi? Bring him here right away or I'll have his head cut off! Surround the house and set fire to it. Let him and his family burn to death. I will destroy anyone who opposes the chanting of the holy names!" (*Caitanya-bhāgavata, Madhya-khaṇḍa* 23.388, 399, 402). When the Kazi realized that he was surrounded by crowds of people carrying flaming torches closing in on him, he knew that there was no way out. In the meantime, some of the devotees were concerned to see how angry Mahāprabhu was and tried to calm Him down. On hearing the devotees' appeal, Chaitanya composed Himself, and His world-destroying Śiva spirit faded away.

Nimāī and the other devotees sat down in front of the Kazi's front door. Nimāī sent one of Navadvīpa's most respected citizens inside to see the Kazi and announce His demands. When the Kazi was assured that Nimāī meant him no harm, he was relieved and came outside. He courteously welcomed Nimāī Paṇḍita to his home and Nimāī answered him with the respect appropriate to a member of the ruling class. They then established a certain intimacy when the Kazi called Nimāī "nephew" and Nimāī responded by calling him "uncle" (*māmā*). In Bengal, everyone has village relations beside their natural family relations. The Kazi came from the same village as Nimāī's mother, Śacī, and as such he was Śacī's village brother and Nimāī's uncle, even though they belonged to mutually exclusive social classes.

In those days, not only would *brāhmaṇas* refuse to speak with Muslims, but, if they were even touched by a Muslim's shadow, they were obliged to take a bath in the Ganges to be purified. It was thus very unusual for the high-caste Nimāī to engage in such a close exchange with the magistrate. The thousands of ordinary people who had come with Nimāī surrounded him and the Muslim magistrate, listening to them intently as they began to discuss various issues.

Nimāī asked why the Kazi had not stopped this huge *kīrtana* on the streets that day. The Kazi eventually explained, "After breaking the *mṛdaṅgas* that day, in the night I had a dream where a furious form sat on my chest: He was half lion and half man. He had His nails on my chest said, 'I will rip apart your chest in exchange for *mṛdaṅgas* that you have broken.' Seeing that form, I closed my eyes and started calling out to Gaurahari, saying, 'Listen, Gaurahari! There will be no more obstacles to the *saṅkīrtana* in Nadiyā. Sing the holy names according to Your desires. If anybody presents an obstacle, I will renounce that person and excommunicate him from the village."

In response to the Kazi, Nimāī explained, "It is everyone's duty to be devoted to God, to think of Him, and to chant His names. Those who engage in *kīrtana* not only repeat God's names, but also think of Him and increase their devotional feelings for Him. By chanting the names of the Lord, all humanity can experience the highest joy and become free from the miseries of material life." Nimāī's charming and humble manner, sweet voice, and deeply reasonable discourse charmed the Kazi. He concluded:

hindūra īśvara baḍa yei nārāyaṇa
sei tumi hao hena laya mora mana

(*Caitanya-caritāmṛta, Ādi-līlā* 17.215)

"The Supreme Deity of the Hindus is Nārāyaṇa. I get the impression that You are this Nārāyaṇa."

The people all watched and waited to hear what Nimāī would say in answer to the Kazi's startling words of praise. Nimāī punctured the charged atmosphere with a laugh. Mahāprabhu gave the Kazi a familiar touch, and began to answer, "You have spoken Kṛṣṇa's name. This is truly wonderful. During our conversation you have uttered the names Kṛṣṇa, Hari, and Nārāyaṇa. You are most fortunate and pious" (*Caitanya-caritāmṛta, Ādi-līlā* 17.216-218).

Of course, it was also unheard of for an ordinary citizen to touch a member of the ruling class in this familiar way. However, the Kazi was so caught up in the emotion of the situation that he had forgotten all about the proper protocol. He simply gazed at Nimāī's beautiful face, his eyes watering, and mentally surrendered himself to His lotus feet. He then prayed to Him for the gift of love of God.

prabhura caraṇa chuṅi' bale priya-vāṇī
tomāra prasāde mora ghucila kumati
ei kṛpā kara yena tomāte rahu bhakti

"He touched Mahāprabhu's lotus feet and spoke sweetly to him, saying: 'My wickedness has been dissipated by Your blessings. Now be kind and bless me again that I may always have devotion to you.'" (*Caitanya-caritāmṛta, Ādi-līlā* 17.219-220) In this way, the prohibition against *kīrtana* was lifted and all the orchestrations of the *pāṣaṇḍīs* were thwarted.

The tomb of Chand Kazi still stands in the village of Bamanpukur not far from Navadvīpa. People of both Hindu and Muslim faiths come there to offer their respects and *salaams* to his memory. It is a true center of unity. Some historians say that this demonstration led by Nimāī in defense of *saṅkīrtana* was the beginning of the Indian freedom movement and the first act of civil disobedience.

The Salvation of Jagāī and Mādhāī

Once the obstacles presented by the Kazi were removed, Nimāī could freely perform *kīrtana* wherever He wanted. As proof of the power of the holy names, many of those very atheists who had been inimical to the chanting were now converted. Significant among these converts were the two brothers Jagāī and Mādhāī. So degraded was this pair that the only sins they had not committed were those that had not yet been invented. They spent all their time in the company of their drunken cronies, but even so, they had been spared the occasion to blaspheme devotees of the Lord. This was their one saving grace.

Lord Kṛṣṇa appeared as the son of Śacī in this present age of Kali to spread the chanting of the holy names. He thus ordered His beloved associates Nityānanda Prabhu (affectionately known as Nitāī) and Haridāsa Ṭhākura to go from door to door to ask people to chant the holy names. One day, as they were going through the town carrying out this order, they happened upon Jagāī and Mādhāī. It was as though destiny had brought them together so that Nitāī, the savior of the most fallen, could shower His mercy upon them.

Nitāī was sometimes called "Avadhūta," which is a type of renunciate who is outside social norms. As soon as Mādhāī heard the word "Avadhūta" pronounced, he became senselessly angry and picked up a piece of a broken pot lying on the ground and hurled it at Nitāī, cutting His forehead. Nitāī's head started to bleed, but rather than becoming angry Himself, He remembered Chaitanya's order and continued glorifying Kṛṣṇa to the two sinful brothers.

In the meantime, Chaitanya, who is present in the soul of all creatures, had become aware of these events and rushed to the scene in the company of His other associates. On seeing Nitāī's wound, He became so angry that He started calling for Sudarśana, His disc-shaped weapon. Mādhāī then fell at Nitāī's feet and begged Him repeatedly for forgiveness. Nitāī is the personification of compassion and so harbored no resentment against Mādhāī; indeed, He forgave him immediately. The two brothers became so remorseful that they promised Nitāī to henceforth stop all sinful activities and commit themselves to the chanting of the holy names and the service of Mahāprabhu's devotees. Chaitanya and all His companions then softened their attitude toward the brothers and absolved them of their transgressions, and, moreover, even destroyed their criminal tendencies.

After being blessed by Nityānanda Prabhu, Jagāī and Mādhāī began to burn with remorse for all the sins they had committed in their lives. They started to keep the company of devotees and commenced an intense regimen of prayer and meditation. They gave up all their evil companions and gradually forgot their past. In time, they both became great devotees. Mahāprabhu even warned His disciples that they should never think less of the two brothers because of their previous immoral activities. Now that they had been transformed, their lives as sinners were to be forgotten. Nityānanda ordered Mādhāī to constantly chant Kṛṣṇa's name and to serve the Ganges River by cleaning the steps leading down to the *ghāṭa*, or bathing place, and to ask everyone for forgiveness, prostrating himself in front of those who came there to bathe. Mādhāī would thus regularly come to the riverbank and remove the accumulated silt and waste with a shovel. Visitors to Navadvīpa still visit this holy site, known as Mādhāī Ghāṭa, today.

This pastime reveals many things about the spiritual path taught by Chaitanya Mahāprabhu. He himself was a *brāhmaṇa* of the highest caste. Haridāsa Ṭhākura, on the other hand, was born in a Muslim family and Nityānanda Prabhu, as an Avadhūta, was outside the caste system. By asking Haridāsa to become the teacher of the holy names, and by saving Jagāī and Mādhāī through Nityānanda Prabhu, Mahāprabhu taught that the teacher of spiritual truth is beyond human designations like caste, class, or race. Through this pastime, He also taught that those who advocate the chanting of the holy names or the teachings of Kṛṣṇa should never do so out of a desire for material profit. There is no greater offense than using God or religion as a business.

There is also a special secret hidden within Mahāprabhu's pastime of calling for His *sudarśana* weapon. Narottama dāsa Ṭhākura taught that even negative emotions such as anger can be used in the service of Kṛṣṇa. He sang, "Use your anger against those who are inimical to Kṛṣṇa (*krodha kṛṣṇa-dveṣi-jane*)." In other words, in certain cases, being angry is not against one's own spiritual welfare. We also see this in the example of Hanumān, the monkey chief of the *Rāmāyaṇa* who served Lord Rāmacandra by showing anger toward the demon Rāvaṇa.

Mahāprabhu Takes Sannyāsa

During the year that Mahāprabhu inaugurated the *saṅkīrtana* movement in Navadvīpa, He performed many wonderful pastimes in the streets and in the homes of its residents. Through these pastimes, He revealed all six traits proclaimed by the Vedic literature to be characteristic of divinity: wealth, bravery, fame, beauty, knowledge, and renunciation.

Then came another event that signaled the turning in Mahāprabhu's life. One day, He was sitting quietly at home, absorbed in the mood of a *gopī*, or cowherd girl, separated from Kṛṣṇa and angry with Him for His lack of compassion in abandoning her. In this state, Mahāprabhu repeated, over and over again, the word "*gopī*, *gopī*." One of His students, a *pāṣaṇḍī*, happened to overhear Him and challenged Him, "Why are You chanting the names of some women instead of the names of Kṛṣṇa? What do You gain by repeating '*gopī*, *gopī*'?" Mahāprabhu thought the student was there to plead on behalf of Kṛṣṇa, towards whom, absorbed in the mood of a *gopī* as He was, He was still feeling angry. He reacted angrily and started to accuse Kṛṣṇa of unfaithfulness and spoke about His flaws. The poor student was completely unable to comprehend Mahāprabhu's words but protested what sounded to him like blasphemy. Mahāprabhu then picked up a stick and started to pursue the boy, who fled in fear of his life. When the student told the other Navadvīpa *brāhmaṇas* what had transpired, they plotted to have some thugs punish Him for His transgression by beating Him.

The inability of the town's *brāhmaṇa* community to understand Him, as well as their reaction to this incident, saddened Mahāprabhu, who spoke the following riddle in response to it:

karila pippali-khaṇḍa kapha nivārite
ulaṭiyā āro kapha bāḍila dehete
(*Caitanya-bhāgavata, Madhya-khaṇḍa* 26.121)

"I took a piece of Indian long pepper (*pipli*) as a medicine for my cough.
But instead of curing my problem, it has simply made my cough worse."

In other words, "I have shown so many wonderful pastimes to teach these people about spiritual life, but they have not been able to understand anything.

Indeed, they are becoming inimical to pure devotion." He concluded that He had to take extraordinary steps to remedy the problem and save them:

ataeva avaśya āmi sannyāsa kariba
sannyāsīra buddhye more praṇata haiba
(*Caitanya-caritāmṛta, Ādi-līlā* 17.265)

> "So, I must take the renounced order of life. If I take *sannyāsa*, people will respect Me simply because of My station in life."

In this way, Mahāprabhu decided to follow the social custom of taking *sannyāsa*. At around the same time, Keśava Bhāratī came through Navadvīpa on his way to his *āśrama* in Katwa. While he was in Navadvīpa, Mahāprabhu served him and revealed to him His intention of taking *sannyāsa*. Thereafter, Keśava Bhāratī went back to Katwa. Nimāī had first shared His idea with Nityānanda Prabhu in private. He told Nityānanda to inform only five people, namely: Śacī Mātā, Gadādhara Paṇḍita, Brahmānanda, Śrī Candraśekhara Ācārya, and Mukunda.

One may ask why Nimāī wanted to take *sannyāsa* when it is known that *sannyāsa* is prohibited in Kali-yuga. The *sannyāsa* which is prohibited is *karma-sannyāsa* and *jñāna-sannyāsa*. However, *sannyāsa* in *bhakti* is always applicable. Here, the Supreme Lord is taking *sannyāsa* to spread loving devotion—*prema-bhakti*. Devotion is eternal. Whatever the Supreme Lord does is beneficial for us. Also, whatever the Supreme Lord does is actual scriptural evidence; all scriptures come from Supreme Lord. Nevertheless, it should be understood that Nimāī's taking *sannyāsa* is not an act that is breaking the prescribed rules of the scriptures. Nimāī takes *sannyāsa* to spread loving devotion to one and all without discrimination.

On the day before Nimāī planned to leave, he spent the entire day in *kīrtana* with His companions. In the evening, he went to the Gaṅgā and offered His obeisance and then went home. Gaurasundara sat at home and all His companions surrounded Him on all four sides. Nobody knew that Nimāī would be leaving; they were happily sitting with Him. His eyes were like lotus petals and His whole body was ornamented with fragrant sandalwood paste and flower garlands. All the Vaiṣṇavas who came to see Him offered sandalwood paste and garlands to Nimāī. Nobody knew where so many people were coming from. Everyone offered obeisance like a stick falling on the ground and then sat down looking at the beautiful face of Nimāī.

Nimāī gave the garlands that were on His neck to all the devotees and instructed them as follows: "Sing the names of Kṛṣṇa. Say, 'Kṛṣṇa,' serve Kṛṣṇa, and sing the names of Kṛṣṇa. Do not think of anything other than Kṛṣṇa. If you have affection for Me, then don't sing anything other than the names of Kṛṣṇa. Whether it be while sleeping, eating, or awake, think of Kṛṣṇa day and night and say His names from your mouth." Thereafter, He told them to all go home. Everybody had *prasāda*. Then, at the end of the day, He returned home, where Śacī Mātā and Viṣṇupriyā were waiting. Viṣṇupriyā brought water to wash His feet, as was the custom. Nimāī went through the customary duties of a householder *brāhmaṇa*—performing His evening meditation and worship, eating sanctified food, and talking with His mother for a while before finally going to His room to rest.

There, the desolate Viṣṇupriyā joined Him. It seemed as though the clouds of imminent separation were gathering in the lonely room. Her anxious questions rumbled like thunder before a storm. The beautiful Viṣṇupriyā herself was like a flash of lightning illuminating Nimāī's body, and finally tears began to pour from her eyes like the rains at the height of the monsoon season. Nimāī asked what was wrong and Viṣṇupriyā told Him how she would not be able to live if Nimāī left and took *sannyāsa*. Nimāī explained to Viṣṇupriyā about how everybody's body is just made of flesh and that the real husband of everybody is Kṛṣṇa. Thereafter, He showed His four-armed Nārāyaṇa form to Viṣṇupriyā Devī.

In the Tretā-yuga when Nimāī had come in the form of Rāmacandra, He had abandoned Sītā Devī and kept her under the care of the sage Vālmīki. Thereafter, Rāmacandra made a golden deity of Sītā Devī in order to perform the required fire sacrifices and worshiped her in a golden form. Therefore, Nimāī explained to Viṣṇupriyā that now she could worship a deity of Himself when He would be gone as a *sannyāsī* in this Kali-yuga. This is described by Śrīla Bhaktivinoda Ṭhākura in *Śrī Navadvīpa Dhāma Māhātmya*, *Parikramā-khānda*, Modadrumadvīpa section.

Nimāī left for Katwa early in the morning. Before leaving, He first offered obeisance to His mother, Śacī Mātā, and circumambulated her. A person should ideally take permission from his mother before going to take *sannyāsa*.

The mother and father are a person's first *gurus*. Even if one takes up the vow of renunciation, he must get the blessings and permission from his elders so that he can be successful in maintaining his vows.

Nityānanda Prabhu, Candraśekhara Ācārya, and Mukunda Datta also went to Katwa following behind Nimāī. Nimāī had spent twenty-four years in Navadvīpa in various wonderful pastimes, and now He was setting off to take *sannyāsa*. The place where Nimāī crossed the Ganges has been immortalized as Nidaya Ghāṭa (a mispronunciation of the actual word, which is *nirdayā*). The word *nirdayā* means "bereft of compassion," for by leaving Navadvīpa, Nimāī seemed to be acting most cruelly to all His family, lifelong friends, and companions. He swam across the Gaṅgā and went towards Katwa, which lies about ten miles to the north on the other bank.

On arriving at Keśava Bhāratī's *āśrama*, Mahāprabhu begged him for *sannyāsa*. His companions had also reached there and stood by and performed *saṅkīrtana* while He danced. A barber was called to shave His head, and as he cut through Mahāprabhu's beautiful tresses, he and all the other devotees shed tears of distress. Colloquially, the barber is known as Madhu Paramanik.

As the day drew to a close, Mahāprabhu whispered a mantra He had received in a dream into Keśava Bhāratī's ear and asked him whether this was indeed the *sannyāsa* mantra. It was Mahāprabhu's wish that Keśava Bhāratī repeat this very same mantra to Him, by speaking it into His ear according to the custom. In fact, by first repeating it to Keśava Bhāratī, Chaitanya Mahāprabhu was in effect blessing him by making him His disciple. Keśava Bhāratī gave Nimāī the name Kṛṣṇa Chaitanya. In His new saffron clothing, Śrī Kṛṣṇa Chaitanya looked extraordinarily beautiful.

The Navadvīpa Residents' Feelings of Separation

Meanwhile, in Navadvīpa, the news quickly spread that Nimāī had left to take *sannyāsa*. Śacī Devī had lost herself in lamentation after the departure of her son. Viṣṇupriyā shed tears incessantly. She felt herself so alone—she was still so young, not yet a woman, and now she was watching the only possibility for future happiness shatter before her eyes. She seemed to have fallen into a shoreless expanse of water, where she was drifting without any direction.

Viṣṇupriyā would have a mood of love in lifelong separation. The intensity of her emotions perhaps even exceeded those of Rādhārāṇī, who suffered so much in a previous age after Kṛṣṇa left for Mathurā. After all, Rādhārāṇī always had the hope that Kṛṣṇa might one day come back, but Viṣṇupriyā could not even hope for that much because her husband had taken *sannyāsa*; after one has taken *sannyāsa*, he can never see his wife. Viṣṇupriyā Devī would set aside a grain rice for each of the *mahā-mantras* that she would chant. At the end of the day, she would cook how many ever grains of rice were set aside while she chanted, offer it to the deity of her husband, and then honor the *prasāda*.

The other devotees in Navadvīpa were also affected by Mahāprabhu's departure. The town was filled with the sounds of their lament, the memory of which still washes over the world, communicating their suffering. The Lord's devotees still look up to the empty sky and sing the words immortalized by Govinda Ghoṣa:

hede re nadiyā vāsi kāra-o mukha cāo
bāhu pasāriyā gorā cāndere phirāo

(Song by Govinda Ghoṣa)

"O citizens of Nadia! To whom will you now turn? Raise your arms to the heavens and pray for our golden moon to come home!"

Festival in Śāntipura

After being ordained a *sannyāsī*, Mahāprabhu left Katwa and was overcome in spiritual ecstasy. He was trying to go to Vṛndāvana. On the way, whoever saw Śrī Kṛṣṇa Chaitanya Mahāprabhu would say "Haribol! Haribol!" and become overcome in divine love. When everyone would say, "Haribol!" upon seeing Him, Mahāprabhu would reply, saying, "I am so grateful to you all for making Me hear the holy names." While Mahāprabhu was attempting to go to Vṛndāvana, Nityānanda Prabhu had another plan. He secretly instructed the cowherd boys to tell Mahāprabhu that the Gaṅgā River was the Yamunā River. Thereafter, Mahāprabhu asked them, "Boys, tell Me which way to go to reach Vṛndāvana." They showed Him the path along the Ganges. Nityānanda

Prabhu instructed Candraśekhara Ācārya to quickly go to Advaita Ācārya's house and arrange a boat. Then He told Candraśekhara Ācārya to call for Śacī Mātā and the devotees to all come to Śāntipura, except for Viṣṇupriyā Devī. Nityānanda then went in front of Mahāprabhu and Mahāprabhu asked him, "Where are You going?" Nityānanda said, "I'm going to Vṛndāvana with You." Mahāprabhu asked him, "How far is Vṛndāvana?" Nityānanda Prabhu replied, "Here is the Yamunā River." He brought Mahāprabhu to the Gaṅgā, but Mahāprabhu couldn't realize that it was the Gaṅgā because He was in devotional ecstasy. Then Mahāprabhu started glorifying the Yamunā while looking at the Gaṅgā and took a bath.

In the meantime, Advaita Ācārya had come with the boat and dry clothes and offered His obeisance. Mahāprabhu became doubtful and said, "Why are You in Vṛndāvana? How did You know that I am here in Vṛndāvana?" Advaita Ācārya said, "Wherever You are, that is Vṛndāvana! It is My fortune that You have come here on the banks of the Gaṅgā." Mahāprabhu then said, "Nityānanda has cheated Me! He has brought Me to the Gaṅgā and said that it is the Yamunā." Advaita Ācārya replied, "Śrīpad Nityānanda didn't lie. You have taken a bath in the Yamunā. Both the Gaṅgā and Yamunā flow together in one stream: the western side is the Yamunā and the eastern side is the Gaṅgā. You've taken Your bath on the western side, which is the Yamunā. You haven't eaten for three days. Come eat in My house today. I've just had some simple food cooked." After this discussion, Mahāprabhu got onto the boat and went to Advaita Ācārya's house. There, Advaita Ācārya had a huge feast prepared for Mahāprabhu. Although Mahāprabhu explained that eating opulently was not good for a *sannyāsī*, Advaita Ācārya explained how He knew Mahāprabhu's true identity, and how Mahāprabhu eats so many preparations in Jagannātha Purī in the form of Jagannātha. Advaita Ācārya also knew the internal reason for Mahāprabhu's taking *sannyāsa* and coming to this world. During this time, Nityānanda Prabhu and Advaita Ācārya had their apparent arguments, yet these arguments took place in order to glorify each other. We should never take sides when Vaiṣṇavas are apparently arguing, because we do not understand the internal reason for their dialogue. As conditioned souls, we get lost in apparent externalities while missing the true essence of the mood of the Vaiṣṇavas. Advaita Ācārya thereafter started massaging Mahāprabhu's feet, but Mahāprabhu was shy and ordered Him to go and take *prasāda*.

The whole day, people were blissful upon seeing the beautiful *sannyāsī* form of Mahāprabhu. In the evening a beautiful *saṅkīrtana* started in Advaita Ācārya's home. Mahāprabhu began to experience ecstatic symptoms and fainted on the ground. Mukunda, who was an extraordinary singer, understood the mood of Mahāprabhu. He knew that Mahāprabhu was experiencing burning separation from Kṛṣṇa and so he began singing appropriate songs. In this way, Mahāprabhu arose and experienced the eight-fold symptoms of ecstasy, including tears, trembling, hairs standing on end, sweating, faltering speech, and so on. He would stand up and then fall to the ground. He experienced indifference, sadness, happiness, pride, humility and so on—it was as if the emotions were fighting a war between each other. He would fall to the ground and stop breathing. He would suddenly jump up and say, "Sing! Sing!" and dance in bliss. Nityānanda would be by Mahāprabhu's side to protect Him. Haridāsa and Advaita Ācārya would be dancing behind Mahāprabhu. Waves of emotions, like happiness and distress, would take over Mahāprabhu. Being overwhelmed in divine love, Mahāprabhu did not even understand His own tiredness. Advaita Ācārya had to stop the *kīrtana* and perform various services for Mahāprabhu to put Him to sleep. In this way, Mahāprabhu stayed at Śāntipura for ten days.

The next morning, Candraśekhara Ācārya brought Śacī Mātā to Śāntipura on a bejeweled palanquin. Mahāprabhu offered His obeisance to His mother and she took Him on her lap and cried out of great affection for her son. Mahāprabhu explained how His body was her own property and that He would stay wherever she instructed. In the meatime, devotees came from so many villages to Śāntipura to see Mahāprabhu. Advaita Ācārya provided living arrangements and food for everyone that came to His home. Śacī Mātā would see her son falling to the ground out of ecstasy during the *kīrtanas* and she would pray to Viṣṇu to protect her son. Śacī Mātā begged everyone to allow her to cook for Mahāprabhu for as long as He would stay at Śāntipura, as this was her only opportunity to see Him. Everyone agreed to the desire of Śacī Mātā.

Mahāprabhu explained that it would not be right for a *sannyāsī* to stay in his home town as society would criticize such a *sannyāsī*; however, He explained that He would never be able to forget His dear Navadvīpa society, just as He would never be able to forget His own mother. Śacī Mātā asked

Mahāprabhu to reside in Jagannātha Purī, where she would be more likely to get news of Him, as devotees would go there from time to time from Bengal. When it was time to go, all the devotees started crying. Nityānanda Prabhu, Jagadānanda Paṇḍita, Dāmodara Paṇḍita, and Mukunda Datta accompanied Mahāprabhu to Purī. Mahāprabhu had also assured Haridāsa Ṭhākura that He would arrange for him to go to Purī and stay there. Advaita Ācārya was following behind and everyone was crying. Mahāprabhu embraced Advaita Ācārya and told Him to please calm all the devotees and His mother down from the deep separation they were feeling from Mahāprabhu. In this way, Mahāprabhu started for Jagannātha Purī.

Raghunātha dāsa Gosvāmī had come to meet Mahāprabhu for the first time in Śāntipura after Mahāprabhu had taken *sannyāsa*. He was overwhelmed in divine love when he offered his obeisance to Mahāprabhu and touched His lotus feet. Raghunātha got to honor the *prasāda* remnants of Mahāprabhu due to the mercy of Advaita Ācārya. He stayed with Mahāprabhu for about five to seven days in Śāntipura, after which Mahāprabhu went to Jagannātha Purī. After going home, Raghunātha dāsa became crazy in divine love and tried in all ways to go to Purī to be with Mahāprabhu; however, his father always kept guards surrounding Raghunātha dāsa so that he could not escape.

Eventually, when Mahāprabhu came back to Śāntipura from Nīlācala during His first attempt to go to Vṛndāvana, Raghunātha dāsa got the opportunity to meet Mahāprabhu at Śāntipura again and at that time, Mahāprabhu told him, "Be steady and don't be crazy. Gradually, you will pass over this ocean of the material world. Don't practice false monkey-like renunciation just to show people of this world. Rather, be involved in your necessary material engagements of the world while being detached. Be completely fixed on the Lord within, but externally, act like a normal materialistic person. Very soon, Kṛṣṇa will deliver you from your material bondages. When I go back to Purī from Vṛndāvana, then come to Me upon some pretext or another. At that time, Kṛṣṇa will be revealed to you. When someone has gotten the mercy of Kṛṣṇa, then who can stop him?"

Worshipper

Part III

Sacred Journeys

Mahāprabhu Arrives in Jagannātha Purī

Mahāprabhu reached Purī in March of 1510. When He first arrived there, He went to see Lord Jagannātha in the temple. The sight of the deity sent Mahāprabhu into an ecstatic trance, and He fell to the ground in a faint. Sārvabhauma Bhaṭṭācārya, a great scholar of Vedānta, happened to be there at the time and, impressed by the young *sannyāsī*, took Him to his own home. The devotees who had accompanied Mahāprabhu revived Him with their chanting of the holy names.

When He returned to consciousness, Sārvabhauma Bhaṭṭācārya proposed that Mahāprabhu take philosophy lessons from him. He would teach Him everything he knew about the monist, or Māyāvāda, philosophy. Mahāprabhu agreed and for seven days the scholar explained the Vedānta *Sūtras* according to Śaṅkara's commentary while Mahāprabhu listened without saying a word. On the eighth day, however, Sārvabhauma became somewhat troubled by Mahāprabhu's silence and asked whether He had any questions. Mahāprabhu responded that though He found the aphorisms of Vyāsadeva very easy to understand, the explanations given by Śaṅkara obscured their crystal-clear meaning. Śaṅkara's commentary, He posited, went against the Vedānta. Lord Śiva appeared as Śaṅkarācārya in the age of Kali to invent this non-dualist philosophy to bewilder the atheists. The true interpretation of the Vedānta is the philosophy of simultaneous oneness and difference. The Māyāvādīs, He said, are disguised atheists:

veda nā māniyā bauddha haya ta nāstika
vedāśraye nāstikya-vāda bauddhake adhika
(*Caitanya-caritāmṛta, Madhya-līlā* 6.168)

"The Buddhists are called atheists because they do not accept the Vedic authority. The Māyāvādīs, however, are worse than the Buddhists, because they preach atheism on the basis of the Vedic literature."

Mahāprabhu proved His point with reference to the scriptures and was able to convince Sārvabhauma Bhaṭṭācārya of His conclusions. After this, Bhaṭṭācārya expressed a desire to hear Mahāprabhu explain a verse from *Śrīmad-Bhāgavatam*: *ātmārāmāś ca munayaḥ* (1.7.10). Mahāprabhu first asked Bhaṭṭācārya to explain his understanding of the verse. Sārvabhauma gave nine possible interpretations, employing his full intellectual prowess and scholarship. After he finished, Mahāprabhu began to give His own explanation. Without even touching on Sārvabhauma's version, He elaborated on its meaning in eighteen different ways, completely astonishing the scholar. Sārvabhauma then surrendered fully to Mahāprabhu, who showered His mercy on him by giving him visions of His various divine forms. Mahāprabhu also blessed him with a clear understanding of the divine truths.

Pilgrimage to South India

A month later, in April of 1510, Mahāprabhu left on pilgrimage to southern India. He wanted to go alone and told all His associates as much. Nityānanda Prabhu insisted, however, that He take a servant. As a result, Mahāprabhu agreed to allow Kṛṣṇadāsa, a *brāhmaṇa*, to accompany Him. Sārvabhauma gave Mahāprabhu a few pieces of cloth and asked Him to stop near the Godāvarī River and meet with Rāmānanda Rāya. Nityānanda and the other devotees went with Mahāprabhu as far as Ālālanātha, where they said their goodbyes.

On the road, Mahāprabhu chanted the holy names in the mood of a *gopī* in separation from Kṛṣṇa. He transformed anyone He encountered into Vaiṣṇavas. It seemed as though Mahāprabhu was being even more merciful to the people of South India than He had been to his neighbors in Navadvīpa, revealing His generosity and compassion to everyone He saw.

When Mahāprabhu arrived at a holy town called Kūrmasthān, He visited the temple of Kūrmadeva and offered the deity prayers and praises. He found lodgings with a local *brāhmaṇa* and, while there, another *brāhmaṇa,* named Vāsudeva Vipra, came to see Him and begged for His mercy. Vāsudeva was seriously ill with leprosy, his body covered with open sores. Mahāprabhu showed His kindness by embracing him and, in so doing, immediately cured him of both his physical and spiritual malaise. He then designated him an *ācārya*, or spiritual teacher, and bestowed on him the name Vāsudeva Amṛtaprada, "Vāsudeva, the giver of immortality."

Mahāprabhu continued on His way to the Godāvarī. Crossing the river, He came to Rajahmundry and from there to Goṣpada Tīrtha. There He observed a man being carried in a palanquin surrounded by numerous *brāhmaṇas* and accompanied by a fanfare of bugles and drums. Recalling the descriptions Sārvabhauma had given Him, Mahāprabhu recognized this person as Rāmānanda Rāya. When Rāmānanda saw the effulgent *sannyāsī* standing by the side of the path, he got down from his elevated seat and prostrated himself on the ground. Mahāprabhu lifted him and embraced him tightly. Waves of divine love rolled over them. Rāmānanda asked Mahāprabhu to stay there for a week or so, so that they could talk about Kṛṣṇa together.

Mahāprabhu found room and board in a *brāhmaṇa's* house. Then, in the evening, Rāmānanda came to see Him dressed in humble attire. He prostrated himself on the ground as a gesture of humility. Mahāprabhu then asked Rāmānanda to explain the purpose of life and the means for attaining it, with reference to the scriptures. Rāmānanda's first answer was that the goal of life is devotion to God, and because God is pleased by the execution of one's duties within the worldly social order, that is the means for attaining the goal of life. This answer failed to satisfy Mahāprabhu, who said it was superficial. Rāmānanda smiled and gave another answer, which again was judged superficial by Mahāprabhu.

One by one, Rāmānanda suggested devotion mixed with fruitive activities, taking shelter of the Lord (*śaraṇāgati*), and devotion mixed with the cultivation of knowledge—only to have each response rejected. Finally, when he arrived at devotion without any hint of the cultivation of knowledge, Mahāprabhu said, "This is correct, but surely you can go even further." Rāmānanda said, "Better than exclusive devotion is devotion in ecstatic love." Mahāprabhu was satisfied with this response also, but nevertheless, Mahāprabhu asked Rāmānanda to go even further. Pressed in this way, Rāmānanda went on to explain love for Kṛṣṇa in the moods of servitude, friendship, guardianship, and finally that of romantic love. The mood of romantic love is present in the spiritual world, where the transcendental milkmaids of Vṛndāvana feel spontaneous love for Kṛṣṇa. In our world, sexuality is an illusory source of happiness, because this world is a perverted reflection of the spiritual world. Thus, everything here is the opposite of its corresponding transcendental image. As such, this mood in love for Kṛṣṇa is elevated and desirable, while the so-called romantic love of this material world proves problematic and unsatisfying.

Mahāprabhu thus accepted love for Kṛṣṇa in the mood of the *gopīs* as the supreme and ultimate mood of devotion. Then Rāmānanda began to glorify Śrīmatī Rādhārāṇī, the best of Kṛṣṇa's mistresses. According to the *Nārada-pañcarātra*, Rādhārāṇī is the queen and presiding deity of the divine *rāsa* dance, where the loving exchange between Kṛṣṇa and the *gopīs* has its ultimate expression.

rāsādhiṣṭhātrī devī ca
svayaṁ rāseśvarī parā
vṛndāvane ca sā devī
paripūrṇatamā satī

"Rādhā is the presiding deity of the *rāsa* dance. She is the queen of the *rāsa* dance. She is the supreme goddess in Vṛndāvana and the most perfect and complete of all chaste women."

The *Nārada-pañcarātra* also states:

yathā brahma-svarūpaś ca
śrī-kṛṣṇaḥ prakṛteḥ paraḥ
tathā brahma-svarūpā sā
nirliptā prakṛteḥ parā

"Just as Kṛṣṇa is the form of Brahman and beyond the material nature, so too is Śrīmatī Rādhārāṇī, who is untouched by matter."

In response to Mahāprabhu's questions, Rāmānanda began to describe the mood of love in separation, finally coming to the *prema-vilāsa-vivarta* at the very highest stage of Rādhārāṇī's love for Kṛṣṇa. As an example of this, he sang a song of his own composition, beginning with the verse:

pahilehi rāga nayana-bhaṅge bhela
anudina bāḍhala avadhi nā gela

"At first, my attraction to Kṛṣṇa arose out of the way he looked at me. From then on, it simply increased, without ever reaching a limit."

After talking about this ultimate stage of divine love, Mahāprabhu asked Rāmānanda how it was possible for an ordinary human being to attain it. Rāmānanda answered that the only way such service could be had is to follow in the footsteps of the *gopīs*. This is the highest possible attainment of human life. Mahāprabhu was very pleased with His conversations with Rāmānanda. Later, Rāmānanda retired from his post as governor and, with the king's permission, came to live in Purī so that he could remain in Mahāprabhu's company.

Thereafter, Mahāprabhu went to Śrī Raṅgam and began to reside at the house of Veṅkaṭa Bhaṭṭa, who was the head priest of the Śrī Raṅgam temple. Mahāprabhu stayed there throughout the four months of the rainy season, when it is prohibited to travel. Mahāprabhu would bathe in the Kāveri River every day and, seeing Lord Raṅganātha, would dance due to being overwhelmed with divine love. Hundreds of thousands of people came to see Mahāprabhu and, by seeing Him, nothing other than the name of Kṛṣṇa came out from their mouths. All the Vaiṣṇava *brāhmaṇas* living in Śrī Raṅgam invited Mahāprabhu for lunch every single day. Despite that, many Vaiṣṇava *brāhmaṇas* did not get the opportunity to serve Mahāprabhu. One Vaiṣṇava *brāhmaṇa* would sit at the Śrī Raṅgam temple and read the *Śrīmad Bhagavad-gītā*. Due to his improper pronunciation, people would laugh at and mock that Vaiṣṇava *brāhmaṇa*. However, that Vaiṣṇava *brāhmaṇa* would be overcome in divine bliss and exhibit the symptoms of ecstasy on his body.

Mahāprabhu asked him what made him so blissful. The Vaiṣṇava *brāhmaṇa* said, "I am a fool. I don't know the meaning of the words or how to read them properly. I am just following the order of my spiritual master. I see Arjuna in the chariot with Kṛṣṇa being the charioteer, speaking the divine instructions. Seeing this scene, I become overcome in bliss. As long as I read, I see this divine sight. For this reason, the words of the *Gītā* do not leave my mind." Mahāprabhu said, "You are the one who is qualified to read the *Gītā*. You know the essential meaning of the *Gītā*." Mahāprabhu embraced the Vaiṣṇava *brāhmaṇa*. The Vaiṣṇava *brāhmaṇa* was crying and, holding Mahāprabhu's feet, said, "Seeing You, I am feeling double the bliss. I feel that You are that Kṛṣṇa Himself." Through the manifestation of Kṛṣṇa in his heart, his heart had become pure; therefore, he was able to know the truth about Mahāprabhu. Mahāprabhu told him not to speak this truth to anyone. That Vaiṣṇava *brāhmaṇa* became Mahāprabhu's devotee and did not leave Mahāprabhu's association throughout the entire four months.

Mahāprabhu continued His pilgrimage through southern India before returning to Purī, where he was given lodging in the house of Kāśī Miśra, the spiritual master of the king himself. Once situated there, Mahāprabhu ordered Nityānanda Prabhu to return to Bengal to inspire and organize His devotees and to preach the holy names far and wide.

King Pratāparudra Pleases Mahāprabhu

At that time, Pratāparudra was the king of Orissa, and Sārvabhauma Bhaṭṭācārya his court scholar. Sārvabhauma was eager to have Mahāprabhu meet the king, but Mahāprabhu was extremely reluctant to do so. According to the rules of behavior for renunciates, it was forbidden for a *sannyāsī* to meet with any materialistic person, and a king was, by definition, the most materialistic of all by virtue of his position alone. As a result, Mahāprabhu refused to entertain any such suggestions. When Rāmānanda Rāya retired from his government service and came to live in Purī, the king acted very sympathetically by not only releasing him from his obligations but awarding him a pension equal to his previous salary as well. Rāmānanda thus praised Pratāparudra to Mahāprabhu, telling him that he was a Vaiṣṇava with all the appropriate qualities. Mahāprabhu's heart softened toward the king after hearing the words of Rāmānanda, but even so, He remained fixed to His principles.

The seasons changed and it came time for *snāna-yātrā*, Lord Jagannātha's annual bathing festival. After the bathing festival, the deity of Lord Jagannātha is kept out of sight of the public for a fortnight. During this time, Mahāprabhu would go to Ālālanātha because He could not tolerate being in Purī while Lord Jagannātha was indisposed. After the two-week period, He returned to Purī and met with Advaita and other devotees from Bengal who had come to see Him and participate in the *ratha-yātrā*.

King Pratāparudra made sure that all the Bengali Vaiṣṇavas were given proper food and accommodation. Out of their appreciation for the king's service, Nityānanda and other devotees asked Mahāprabhu to grant him an audience. When Mahāprabhu remained intransigent, Nityānanda had to pacify the king by giving him a piece of Mahāprabhu's used cloth. Rāmānanda then arranged for Mahāprabhu to meet the adolescent crown prince, whom Mahāprabhu embraced as a Vaiṣṇava. Mahāprabhu's touch sent the prince into a convulsion of ecstasy, and later, when King Pratāparudra touched his son, he too experienced the power of Mahāprabhu's blessings and divine love.

Finally, it was time for the *ratha-yātrā* festival. According to the ancient custom, King Pratāparudra swept the ground before Lord Jagannātha's chariot with a gold-handled broom, and then sprinkled it with sandalwood-scented water. Chaitanya Mahāprabhu observed how the king performed this service in genuine humility and was very pleased.

During the pulling of the chariots, Mahāprabhu became absorbed in chanting and dancing, as always. When the chariots stopped at the midpoint between the temple and Guṇḍicā, their destination, Mahāprabhu rested in a shaded garden called Balagaṇḍi. He was still overcome by the ecstasies of the festival and only half aware of what was going on around Him. At this time, King Pratāparudra, dressed simply as a Vaiṣṇava, approached Mahāprabhu alone and began to massage His feet. At the same time, he recited the verses from the Śrīmad-*Bhāgavatam* known as "The Song of the Gopīs." The following verse was especially dear to Mahāprabhu:

tava kathāmṛtaṁ tapta-jīvanaṁ
kavibhir īḍitaṁ kalmaṣāpaham

śravaṇa-maṅgalaṁ śrīmad-ātataṁ
bhuvi gṛṇanti ye bhūridā janāḥ
(*Śrīmad-Bhāgavatam* 10.31.9, *Caitanya-caritāmṛta, Madhya-līlā* 14.14)

> My Lord, Your words and the descriptions of Your activities are like nectar for those who have been made thirsty in this desert-like material world. Transmitted by exalted personalities, these narrations eradicate all sinful reactions. Whoever hears them attains all good fortune. Those in this world who broadcast these delightful topics are certainly the most munificent altruists.

As soon as Mahāprabhu heard this verse, he embraced the king. Mahāprabhu recognized him as a genuine humble Vaiṣṇava and no longer saw him as the icon of materialistic culture.

Pilgrimage to Vṛndāvana

Not long afterward, Mahāprabhu set off on a pilgrimage to Vṛndāvana. He decided to follow the route along the Ganges, which flows through Bengal. Some legends say that He stopped at Śāntipura on this trip and saw His mother for the last time, for Mahāprabhu would never again set foot in the land of His birth. He reached Rāmakeli, a village near the capital city, where He met Rūpa and Sanātana Gosvāmis for the first time. These two brothers were well-known ministers in the government of the ruler, Hussein Shah. Under the influence of Mahāprabhu, Rūpa and Sanātana soon gave up their ministerial service and accepted the renounced order of life.

From there, Mahāprabhu continued His journey. He did not want to take anybody along this time. However, upon the repeated requests of Svarūpa Dāmodara and Rāya Rāmānanda, Mahāprabhu agreed to take Balabhadra Bhaṭṭācārya along with Balabhadra Bhaṭṭācārya's servant. Mahāprabhu took permission from Lord Jagannātha and started on His journey in the middle of the night when everyone was asleep. The next morning, everyone was searching for Mahāprabhu, and, not finding Him anywhere, they became overwhelmed in distress. Svarūpa Dāmodara pacified everyone, and they all understood the Lord's desire. Meanwhile, Chaitanya Mahāprabhu walked on the path which was not usually walked on by the public. Keeping Cuttack on His right, He entered the forest and starting walking through, chanting the names of Kṛṣṇa. The elephants, tigers, and wild boars moved out of the way when Mahāprabhu was walking. Balabhadra was in fear watching this sight. One day, a tiger was sleeping in the path and Mahāprabhu's foot touched the tiger as He was in ecstasy. Then Mahāprabhu told the tiger, "Say Kṛṣṇa." The tiger started dancing while saying "Kṛṣṇa! Kṛṣṇa!" One day, Mahāprabhu was bathing in a river; an elephant came in front of Him and Mahāprabhu threw some water on the elephant, telling the elephant, "Say Kṛṣṇa!" Whichever beings were touched by even a drop of the water thrown by Mahāprabhu all began singing "Kṛṣṇa! Kṛṣṇa!" and dancing in divine love. Through His chanting, wild tigers and elephants began dancing and chanting the names of Kṛṣṇa in the ecstasy of divine love!

Mahāprabhu Dances with Tigers and Deer

Mahāprabhu remembered Vṛndāvana while walking in the jungle. Tigers and deer began walking along with Him as He chanted descriptions from the *Śrīmad-Bhāgavatam* about Vṛndāvana and the fortunate animals therein. Whenever Mahāprabhu told the deer and tigers to chant "Kṛṣṇa!" they would immediately chant the names of Kṛṣṇa, sing, dance, and cry. The tigers and deer would embrace each other and kiss each other's faces. The peacocks and birds went along with Mahāprabhu and became intoxicated by chanting "Kṛṣṇa! Kṛṣṇa!" and dancing. When Mahāprabhu would say, "Haribol!" the trees and plants swelled with life. All the moving and non-moving living entities in the Jhārikhaṇḍa forest became intoxicated due to Mahāprabhu giving them the name of Kṛṣṇa. The people of whichever village Mahāprabhu traveled through received *prema-bhakti*, divine loving service for Kṛṣṇa. Whoever heard the names of Kṛṣṇa from Mahāprabhu's mouth would tell the name to others and those other people would in turn give the holy names to other people.

In this way, everyone was chanting "Kṛṣṇa! Hari!" dancing, crying, and laughing in ecstasy. Everyone of the entire land became Vaiṣṇavas through the *paramparā* system of receiving the holy name from Mahāprabhu to person to person. People became Vaiṣṇavas just by seeing Mahāprabhu. Mahāprabhu personally traveled throughout India in this way and delivered everyone. The people of Jhārikhaṇḍa were especially degraded, but Mahāprabhu specifically went on that route towards Vṛndāvana to deliver those people. Wherever He saw a forest, He thought it was Vṛndāvana; wherever He saw a mountain, He thought it was Govardhana. Wherever He saw a river, He thought it was the Kālindi Yamunā. In this way, Mahāprabhu danced, cried, and fell to the ground in extreme ecstasy of Kṛṣṇa-prema. Mahāprabhu was so happy having come on the forest path rather than the path traveled by most people. On this route there would be no obstacles created by large crowds while going to Vṛndāvana. He said, "Kṛṣṇa is an ocean of mercy and especially compassionate upon the lowly and fallen. Without the mercy of Kṛṣṇa, there is no happiness."

Mahāprabhu Pacifies the Vārāṇasī Sannyāsīs

Upon reaching Kāśī (Vārāṇasī), Mahāprabhu took a bath at Maṇikarṇikā Ghāṭa and there, Tapana Miśra saw Him. Tapana Miśra had seen Mahāprabhu earlier in Bangladesh, but this was the first time Tapana Miśra was seeing Mahāprabhu as a *sannyāsī*. He fell at Mahāprabhu's feet, crying, and Mahāprabhu picked Tapana Miśra up and embraced him. They went to see Viśvanātha and Bindu Mādhava and then went to Tapana Miśra's house, wherein Tapana Miśra began dancing in joy. Tapana Miśra invited Mahāprabhu to his home and once there washed His feet and worshiped Mahāprabhu as well as Balabhadra Baṭṭācārya. Balabhadra Bhaṭṭātacārya then cooked a meal for Mahāprabhu. After taking His meal, Mahāprabhu took rest and Tapana Miśra's son, Raghunātha, massaged Mahāprabhu's divine feet. The entire Miśra family honored the remnants of Mahāprabhu's meal. Hearing that Mahāprabhu had come to Vārāṇasī, Candraśekhara arrived. Candraśekhara was Tapana Miśra's friend. He used to write and was of the doctor caste. Candraśekhara fell at Mahāprabhu's feet and began crying and Mahāprabhu embraced him. Candraśekhara expressed how everyone in Vārāṇasī would only speak about *māyā* and *brahma* and the six philosophical *darśanas*; only Tapana Miśra would speak about Kṛṣṇa. Thus, these two dear servants of Mahāprabhu begged Him to stay and deliver them. Although Mahāprabhu wanted to go to Vṛndāvana, He was subjugated by the love of Tapana Miśra and Candraśekhara and stayed in Vārāṇasī for ten days. Tapana Miśra requested Mahāprabhu to stay in his house throughout the stay in Vārāṇasī.

A Maharashtrian *brāhmaṇa* came to see Mahāprabhu and was amazed by seeing the divine form and love that Mahāprabhu possessed. All the *brāhmaṇas* invited Mahāprabhu for lunch but, knowing them to be *māyāvādīs* and non-Vaiṣṇavas, Mahāprabhu would never go to them. Instead, He would thus say, "I have already had my meal today." He would not associate with the *sannyāsīs* there. There was a famous Vedānta teacher in Vārāṇasī known as Prakāśānanda Sarasvatī. One day, a *brāhmaṇa* went to Prakāśānanda and started describing Mahāprabhu. He said, "A *sannyāsī* has come from Jagannātha Purī and I am unable to describe His glories and power. Whatever I see in Him is quite amazing. He is very tall and broad and has a pure golden complexion. His arms reach down to His knees and His eyes are the shape of lotus petals. He seems to have all the qualities of God. When I see Him, I think, 'This is Nārāyaṇa.' Whoever sees Him starts singing the names of Kṛṣṇa. I heard from the *Bhāgavatam* that these are all the signs of a *mahābhāgavata*. His tongue is unendingly singing the names of Kṛṣṇa and streams of tears flow from His eyes like the Gaṅgā. He dances, laughs, sings, cries, and loudly roars like a lion. The whole world becomes auspicious. His name is Kṛṣṇa Chaitanya. His name, form, and qualities are incomparable. Seeing Him, it's clear that He is God, but who will believe His transcendental activities?"

Prakāśānanda heard this and laughed, saying, "The *sannyāsīs* from Gauḍadeśa, Bengal, are sentimental and emotional. He is a disciple of Keśava Bhāratī. He wanders from village to village dancing. Whoever seems Him says that He is God. It is an art of illusion. The toughest scholar, Sārvabhauma Bhaṭṭācārya, became crazy by associating with this Chaitanya. Saying that He is a *sannyāsī* is just a trick. His sentimental and emotional acts will not influence anyone in Vārāṇasī. Don't go near Him; rather, listen to Vedānta. If you associate with such upstarts, you will be destroyed."

Hearing the words of Prākaśānanda, that *brāhmaṇa* felt very sad and started saying, "Kṛṣṇa, Kṛṣṇa." The *brāhmaṇa's* mind had become purified already, as he had seen Mahāprabhu. He went to Mahāprabhu and explained what had happened. Hearing this, Mahāprabhu laughed. The *brāhmaṇa* said, "When I said Your name, Prākaśānanda already knew it and said Your name Mahāprabhu himself. To point out faults in You, he said Your name, 'Chaitanya,' three times. However, the name 'Kṛṣṇa' did not come out of his mouth. He said Your name out of scorn, and that made me feel sad. Please tell me the reason for this. When I see You, my mouth automatically says, 'Kṛṣṇa, Hari.'"

Mahāprabhu replied, "Māyāvādis offend Kṛṣṇa. They constantly say, '*brahma*,' '*ātma*,' and 'Chaitanya.' Thus, the name 'Kṛṣṇa' does not come out of their mouths. The name of Kṛṣṇa and Kṛṣṇa Himself are equal. The name, the deity, and the Lord Himself are one; there is no difference between these three. All three are transcendental bliss. There is no difference between Kṛṣṇa and His name. There is no difference between Kṛṣṇa and His body. For the embodied souls, there is a difference between their names, bodies, and true forms. Therefore, Kṛṣṇa's name, body, and pastimes cannot be understood through material senses; rather they are self-manifested and revealed. Kṛṣṇa's names, qualities, and pastimes are equivalent to Kṛṣṇa Himself: they are all transcendental. When the soul, in its true spiritual constitutional position, turns towards Kṛṣṇa, then through the transcendental senses, Kṛṣṇa's names, qualities, pastimes, and so on will become self-manifest and reveal themselves. The nectarine pastimes of Kṛṣṇa are more blissful than the bliss that is present in the formless Brahman. The pastimes even attract great scholars on the path of impersonal realization. We offer our obeisance to Śukadeva Gosvāmī, the son of Vyāsa, who was at first a scholar of impersonal realization but later became attracted by the sweet pastimes of Kṛṣṇa and spoke the *Śrīmad-Bhāgavata Purāṇa*. Because Kṛṣṇa's qualities are more blissful than the bliss that is present in the formless Brahman, these qualities even attract those who are liberated and take delight in the self (*ātmārāmā*). Those liberated personalities are attracted by the divine lotus feet of Kṛṣṇa. What to speak of the feet, they become attracted by the fragrance of the Tulasī leaves, which ornament the divine lotus feet of Kṛṣṇa. Therefore, the name of Kṛṣṇa does not come into the mouths of Māyāvādīs, as they are turned totally away from Kṛṣṇa. I came to Vārāṇasī to give out this love of Kṛṣṇa, but it seems there are no buyers, and I should just go back home. I brought such a heavy burden on My back and now how will I take it with Me and go? I will distribute it even for a small price (meaning an intense longing for it born of surrender)." The *brāhmaṇa* absorbed these teachings.

Passing through Prayāga

The next morning, Mahāprabhu left for Mathurā. Tapana Miśra, Candraśekhara, and the *brāhmaṇa* wanted to accompany Mahāprabhu, but Mahāprabhu forbade them and sent them home. Mahāprabhu continued on His way to Vṛndāvana. The three of them felt great separation from Mahāprabhu and became intoxicated in transcendental emotions while discussing Mahāprabhu's wonderful qualities. Mahāprabhu reached Prayāga and took a bath in the river. He saw Veṇī-Mādhava in the temple and danced and sang in ecstasy. Seeing the Yamunā, Mahāprabhu became overwhelmed and jumped into the river. Balabhadra Bhaṭṭācārya quickly went and lifted Mahāprabhu out of the water. In this way, Mahāprabhu stayed in Prayāga for three days and delivered the people there by giving out the names of Kṛṣṇa and divine love. In the same way, Mahāprabhu delivered everyone He saw on the way to Mathurā. All the people danced in bliss just like those who had been delivered in southern and western India through Mahāprabhu's travels there. Wherever Mahāprabhu would see the Yamunā, He would jump into the water and faint in spiritual bliss.

Arrival in Mathurā

As they approached Mathurā, Mahāprabhu fell to the ground like a stick and offered His obeisance, having become overwhelmed in love of Kṛṣṇa. Upon entering Mathurā, Mahāprabhu took a bath at Viśrāma Ghāṭa. He offered obeisance to Keśava at His birthplace. Mahāprabhu danced, sang, and loudly roared, being submerged in spiritual ecstasies. Everyone who saw this sight was amazed. One *brāhmaṇa* fell at Mahāprabhu's divine feet and started dancing with Mahāprabhu, and he also became overwhelmed in divine love. They both danced and hugged each other. They raised their arms, chanting, "Hari! Kṛṣṇa!" All the surrounding people began chanting "Hari! Hari!" and the holy names loudly resonated in the atmosphere. There, the servant of the deity Keśava offered a garland to Mahāprabhu. People were amazed and said, "We have never seen such transcendental activities before. They are not of this world. When someone sees Mahāprabhu, they become intoxicated in divine love and begin to laugh, cry, dance, and sing while chanting Kṛṣṇa's names. It is unequivocally clear that He is Kṛṣṇa and He has come to Mathurā to deliver the residents."

Thereafter, Mahāprabhu took that *brāhmaṇa* aside and privately asked him, "Gentleman, you are very simple and an aged *brāhmaṇa*. From where did you receive this treasure of ecstatic love?" The *brāhmaṇa* said, "Śrīpad Mādhavendra Purī traveled and traveled and one day came to Mathurā. He mercifully came to my place of residence, accepted me as his disciple, and even had a meal cooked by me. Mādhavendra Purī established the worship of Gopāla and till this day, Gopāla is being served on Govardhana." Hearing this, Mahāprabhu offered his prayers to the *brāhmaṇa* and the *brāhmaṇa*, out of fear, fell at Mahāprabhu's feet. Mahāprabhu said, "You are the *guru* and I am like your disciple. It is not proper for the *guru* to offer obeisance to the disciple." The *brāhmaṇa* was surprised and fearful and said, "Why do You speak in this way as a *sannyāsī*? However, seeing Your divine love, I surmise that You are linked with Mādhavendra Purī. Such love can only exist where there is some connection with Mādhavendra Purī. Otherwise, not even the slightest fragrance of such love can exist." Then, Balabhadra Bhaṭṭācārya explained the connection. The *brāhmaṇa* became so blissful hearing about it that he began dancing. Then, the *brāhmaṇa* brought Mahāprabhu to his home and offered many different services to Mahāprabhu.

The *brāhmaṇa* was from a family of gold merchants (the Sanoḍiyā division of *brāhmaṇas*) and since that profession causes them to become impure, *sannyāsīs* do not eat at their homes despite their being *brāhmaṇas*. The *brāhmaṇa* asked Balabhadra Bhaṭṭācārya to cook for Mahāprabhu. However, Mahāprabhu laughed and said, "Mādhavendra Purī Gosāi ate in your house. It is my instruction that you cook for Me." Even though he was a Sanoḍiyā, he was still a *brāhmaṇa* and even though *sannyāsīs* do not eat in the home of Sanoḍiyās, Mādhavendra Purī saw this *brāhmaṇa's* Vaiṣṇava qualities and behavior, accepted him as a disciple, and ate in his house. When Mahāprabhu told the *brāhmaṇa* that He would eat in his house, the *brāhmaṇa*, out of great humility, spoke, "It is my great fortune that I can serve You a meal. You are the Supreme Lord and You are not bound to follow any rules of behavior. However, foolish people will criticize You and I will be unable to tolerate those peoples' critical words." Mahāprabhu replied, "The *smṛti* scriptures, *śruti* scriptures, and all the sages have differing views on *dharma*. It is the duty of the *sādhu* (one who is truly searching out the Absolute Truth) to establish *dharma* through his behavior. Mādhavendra Purī Gosāī's behavior is the essence of all *dharma*." It is proper to follow the path shown by the pure devotees. The *brāhmaṇa* then offered food to Mahāprabhu in his home and all the people of Mathurā came to see Mahāprabhu.

Hundreds of thousands of people, an uncountable number of people, arrived and Mahāprabhu came out of the house to allow them to see Him. He lifted His arms and said, "Haribol!" Everyone became intoxicated in divine love and danced; the whole atmosphere resounded with the sound of "Hari." Mahāprabhu took baths at the twenty-four *ghāṭas* of the Yamunā river and the *brāhmaṇa* showed Mahāprabhu all the pastime places of Kṛṣṇa. Mahāprabhu saw Svāyambhu Viśrama, Dīrghaviṣṇu, Bhūteśvara, Mahāvidyā, and Gokarṇeśvara. Mahāprabhu took the Sanoḍiyā *brāhmaṇa* along with Him to see Madhuvana, Tālavana, Kumudavana and Bahulāvana. Mahāprabhu bathed in all these forests and was overwhelmed with transcendental emotions.

Mahāprabhu Exhibits Pastimes of Divine Love

When the cowherd men were herding their cows, the cows surrounded Mahāprabhu as soon as they saw Him. Seeing the cows, Mahāprabhu was stunned and waves of transcendental bliss overtook Him. The cows in turn began to lick Mahāprabhu out of parental love. Mahāprabhu regained His composure and petted the cows, lovingly rubbing His hands along their bodies. The cows proceeded to follow Mahāprabhu when He continued walking. With great difficulty, the cowherd men brought the cows back and prevented them from going with Mahāprabhu. Hearing Mahāprabhu's voice, many deer also began coming to Him. The bucks and does saw Mahāprabhu and began licking His body. They fearlessly followed Mahāprabhu on all the paths He took. The parrots, cuckoos, and bees sang the fifth musical note (*pa*) when they saw Him. The peacocks danced and went ahead of Mahāprabhu. The trees and plants of Vṛndāvana bloomed in delight and cried tears of honey. They became filled with flowers and fruits, which then fell on Mahāprabhu's divine feet. It was just like friends exchanging gifts after a reunion. All the moving and stationary living entities of Vṛndāvana were in bliss, just as one feels upon seeing his dear friends.

Seeing their love, Mahāprabhu became overwhelmed in divine emotions. He played with everyone and was subjugated by their love. Mahāprabhu embraced every tree and plant. Mahāprabhu offered all the flowers and fruits to Kṛṣṇa through meditation. Mahāprabhu's body was restless; tears flowed from His eyes, His body was trembling, and His hairs were standing on end. He loudly exclaimed, "Say, 'Kṛṣṇa'! Say, 'Kṛṣṇa'!" All the moving and stationary living entities of Vṛndāvana, as if an echo of Mahāprabhu's deep voice, unitedly chanted "Kṛṣṇa!" in response.

Mahāprabhu held the neck of a deer and cried. The hairs of the deer stood on end in delight and tears flowed from its eyes. Mahāprabhu saw a male and a female parrot on a tree branch. The parrots flew and sat on His hand and began to describe the glories of Kṛṣṇa and Rādhikā. The male parrot said, "Let my Lord Kṛṣṇa, who is the Lord of entire universe and the enchanter of all, maintain the universe. His beauty steals away the patience of all women. His pastimes astound Lakṣmī Devī. His strength makes the Govardhana mountain seem like a toy ball. His pure qualities are transcendentally unlimited. His character gives joy to one and all."

The female parrot replied, "Śrīmatī Rādhikā's love, beautiful form, character, expertise in dancing and singing, poetic prowess, and so on enchants even the mind of the one who enchants the entire universe. Thus, She gains even more beauty." The male parrot said, "Kṛṣṇa enchants even Cupid, O female parrot. May that Madana Mohana, who holds the *vaṁśi* flute, who enchant the hearts of all the women of the world and who enjoys pastimes with the damsels of Vraja, always be victorious!" The female parrot mocked the male parrot, saying, "When Kṛṣṇa gains beauty by being with Rādhikā, then He enchants Cupid as Madana Mohana. However, if Kṛṣṇa does not stay with Rādhikā, then even though He enchants the whole universe, Kṛṣṇa will become enchanted by Cupid." Hearing this, Mahāprabhu was astonished and experienced great delight. The parrots flew back onto the tree branch. Mahāprabhu joyfully watched the peacocks dancing. Seeing the color of the peacocks' throat, Mahāprabhu remembered Kṛṣṇa's complexion and fell on the ground, overwhelmed in divine love.

The *brāhmaṇa* and Balabhadra Bhaṭṭācārya saw that Mahāprabhu had fainted and served Him with great care. They quickly took Mahāprabhu's external cloth, which was on top of His body, and used it to fan Him. They sprinkled water on His body as well. They loudly chanted the name of Kṛṣṇa in Mahāprabhu's ear. Mahāprabhu regained consciousness and began rolling on the ground. His body was afflicted by the thorns that filled the forests. Balabhadra Bhaṭṭācārya took Mahāprabhu on his lap and carefully healed Him. Mahāprabhu was absorbed in remembrance of Kṛṣṇa. His mind was restless. He loudly said, "Chant! Chant!" as He stood up and danced. Balabhadra Bhaṭṭācārya and the *brāhmaṇa* sang the names of Kṛṣṇa as Mahāprabhu danced along the path. The *brāhmaṇa* was astonished seeing Mahāprabhu's elevated state and worried about His protection.

Mahāprabhu was one hundred times more overwhelmed in divine love on His way to Mathurā than He was in Nīlācala Jagannātha Purī. In Mathurā itself, Mahāprabhu was a thousand times more overwhelmed, and while wandering in the forests, His feelings multiplied by a hundred thousand times. While in other places, He would brim with transcendental bliss merely upon hearing the name of Vṛndāvana; but now, Mahāprabhu was wandering in Vṛndāvana itself. His mind was restless day and night; He took baths, ate, and did His normal duties just out of practice. Such were His exhibitions of ecstasy while wandering through the twelve forests. This is just a summary of Mahāprabhu's transformations; even millions of books on the topic cannot describe His feelings in Vṛndāvana. The entire world was floating in the ocean of the pastimes of Chaitanya Mahāprabhu. One would swim as much as was his ability to do so in this ocean of divine pastimes.

Mahāprabhu Visits Kṛṣṇa's Pastime Places

In this manner, Mahāprabhu danced and danced and gained external awareness upon reaching Arata village. Mahāprabhu asked the local people about the location of Rādhā-kuṇḍa but no one seemed to know where it was; neither did the Sanoḍiyā *brāhmaṇa* who was accompanying Him. Mahāprabhu, being the Supreme Lord, knew that Rādhā-kuṇḍa was lost over time. He took baths in two small bodies of water in a paddy field. The villagers watched in amazement. Mahāprabhu began praising Rādhā-kuṇḍa: "Amongst all *gopīs*, Rādhā is most loved by Kṛṣṇa. In the same way, this Rādhā-kuṇḍa is most dear to Kṛṣṇa, as it is the liquid water form of His beloved. Kṛṣṇa eternally plays with Rādhikā in the waters of Rādhā-kuṇḍa and dances with Her on the banks of Rādhā-kuṇḍa. Kṛṣṇa gives divine love just like Rādhā's love to one who once takes a bath in Rādhā-kuṇḍa. The sweetness of Rādhā-kuṇḍa is like Rādhā's sweetness. The glories of Rādhā-kuṇḍa are like Rādhā's glories." Offering praise in this manner, Mahāprabhu became overwhelmed in spiritual ecstasy. He danced on the banks of Rādhā-kuṇḍa while remembering the pastimes of Rādhā and Kṛṣṇa which happen at Rādhā-kuṇḍa. Mahāprabhu applied a *tilaka* on His forehead with the mud of Rādhā-kuṇḍa and had Balabhadra Bhaṭṭācārya take some mud along with them on their journey.

Mahāprabhu then arrived at Sumanaḥ Sarovara (Kusuma Sarovara). From there, He saw Govardhana and became overwhelmed. Seeing Govardhana as Harideva (non-different from Kṛṣṇa), He offered obeisance. On the western petal of the lotus-shaped region of Mathurā resided Harideva, who is the primary expansion of Nārāyaṇa. Mahāprabhu was intoxicated in divine love and danced in front of Harideva. After hearing about the amazing activities of Mahāprabhu, all the people came to see what was happening. Everyone was astonished upon seeing the beauty of Mahāprabhu. Mahāprabhu worshiped the servant of Harideva. Balabhadra Bhaṭṭācārya then cooked a meal at Brahma-kuṇḍa, where Mahāprabhu bathed and then ate. That night, Mahāprabhu stayed at Harideva's temple. During the night, He began thinking, "I will never climb on top of Govardhana. How will I see Gopāla Rāya?" Thinking in this way, Mahāprabhu remained silent. Gopāla knew Mahāprabhu's mind and arranged the pretext of fear of attack from the Muslims. Mahāprabhu was in the mood of a devotee and thought that He should not climb on Govardhana. As a result, Gopāla Himself came down to see Mahāprabhu. Gopāla was staying in a village known as Annakūta. The Rājputa people stayed in that village. In the night, one person came and told the village people, "The Muslims are coming to destroy your village. Leave tonight without leaving behind even one person. Take Gopāla and leave from here; the Muslims are coming tomorrow." Hearing this, the villagers became worried. They first took Gopāla and hid Him in Gāṅṭhuli village. There, Gopāla was served secretly in a *brāhmaṇa's* house. The Annakūta village was destroyed, and all the people fled. In this manner, Gopāla went from place to place on the pretext of fear of the Muslims.

In the morning, Mahāprabhu bathed in Mānasī-Gaṅgā and began to circumambulate Govardhana. Seeing Govardhana, Mahāprabhu was overcome with love. He danced and danced and recited a verse from the *Śrīmad-Bhāgavatam* describing Govardhana: "Govardhana Mountain is the topmost Vaiṣṇava because he swells in joy by the touch of the divine feet of Balarāma and Kṛṣṇa and then gives drinking water, grass, fruits, roots, etc., to Rādhā and Kṛṣṇa, as well as to Their associates." Thereafter, Mahāprabhu took a bath in Govinda-kuṇḍa. There, He heard that Gopāla was now in Gāṅṭhuli village. Mahāprabhu went to that village and saw Gopāla. Mahāprabhu sang the holy names and danced in the ecstasy. Mahāprabhu was overwhelmed seeing Gopāla's beauty. Mahāprabhu danced and danced till the end of the day, reciting a verse from the *Bhakti-rasamrta-sindhu*: "May the left arm of Kṛṣṇa protect you, that left arm of the lotus-eyed Śrī Kṛṣṇa who lifted Girirāja like a play ball." Like this, Mahāprabhu saw Gopāla for three days. On the fourth day, Gopāla went to His temple. The people accompanied Gopāla with singing and dancing and the blissful atmosphere resounding with the sound of "Hari! Hari"! Gopāla went into His temple on the top of Govardhana but Mahāprabhu stayed at the foot of Govardhana Mountain. Gopāla had fulfilled the desires of Mahāprabhu. Gopāla is very merciful and compassionate by nature and He desires to see His own devotees. Mahāprabhu was anxious to see Gopāla but had resolved to not climb on Govardhana Mountain; as a result, Gopāla made a pretext upon which He could come down from the top of Govardhana Mountain. Gopāla sometimes stays in forest groves and sometimes in villages and devotees come to see Gopāla wherever He is situated.

Thereafter, Mahāprabhu went to Kāmyavana, and He traveled there in the same ecstatic manner along the paths, as described earlier. Mahāprabhu saw the places of Kṛṣṇa's pastimes therein and then went to Nandīśvara (the area of Nanda Mahārāja's home). Seeing Nandīśvara, Mahāprabhu became overcome with bliss. Then, He took a bath in Pāvana-sarovara. He asked the local people, "Is there a deity on the top of the mountain?" The people replied, "There are deities inside a cave. There is a mother and father and in between them is a beautiful child with a three-fold-bending form." Hearing this, Mahāprabhu became blissful and saw the three deities inside the cave. Mahāprabhu offered obeisance to the divine feet of Vrajendra (Nanda Maharāja) and Vrajeśvari (Yaśodā Maiyā). In ecstatic transcendental love, Mahāprabhu touched the whole body of Kṛṣṇa. Mahāprabhu spent every day being overwhelmed in divine love, dancing, and singing.

From there, Mahāprabhu went to Khadirivana. He saw the places of Kṛṣṇa's pastimes there and then went to Śeṣa-śāyī. He saw Lakṣmī Devī there and recited a verse spoken by the *gopīs* from the *Śrīmad-Bhāgavatam*: "O beloved! We slowly hold Your soft feet on our hard breasts. Now You are wandering in the forests with those same feet and those feet will surely be cut by small stones and rocks, which cause You pain. You are our very lives, and thus our minds have become unstable and worried thinking about You." Then, Mahāprabhu saw Khela-tīrtha and then moved onto Bhāṇḍirvana. From there, He crossed the Yamunā and went to Bhadravana. Next, Mahāprabhu went to Śrīvana (Belvana) and then on to Lohavana. Thereafter, He went to Mahāvana and saw the birthplace of Kṛṣṇa in Gokula. Mahāprabhu saw the place where the Yamalārjuna trees fell and He was overwhelmed in divine love and His mind became unstable. After seeing Gokula, Mahāprabhu went to Mathurā. There, He saw the birthplace of Kṛṣṇa and then stayed in the house of the Sanoḍiyā *brāhmaṇa* who was a disciple of Mādhavendra Purī. Seeing huge crowds of people, Mahāprabhu left Mathurā and went to Akrūra-tīrtha and stayed there. After some days, Mahāprabhu went to see Vṛndāvana. There He bathed at Kālīya-hrada and at the Praskandana holy place. Then, from the Dvādaśāditya place, Mahāprabhu went to Keśī-tīrtha. He saw the Rāsa-sthalī and fainted in ecstasy. After regaining consciousness, Mahāprabhu again began rolling on the ground. He was laughing, crying, dancing, falling, and singing at a high pitch. In this manner, that day passed. In the evening, Mahāprabhu came back to Akrūra-tīrtha and had His meal there.

In the morning, Mahāprabhu bathed at Cira-ghāṭa and rested at the tamarind tree, Teṅtulī-talā (Imlītalā). The tree there is from the time of Kṛṣṇa's pastimes. The Yamunā flowed nearby with a cool breeze. The Lord watched the beauty of Vṛndāvana and the waters of the Yamunā. Mahāprabhu sat at the Teṅtulī-talā and chanted the holy names of Kṛṣṇa. He performed His afternoon prayers and then went to Akrūra-tīrtha for His meal. Many people came to see Mahāprabhu at Akrūra-tīrtha; due to the crowd, Mahāprabhu could not chant the holy names as He desired to do methodically, keeping count. Mahāprabhu then went to Vṛndāvana and sat in a solitary place and chanted the holy names until the afternoon. In the afternoon (third *prahara*, nine hours after sunrise), people came to see Mahāprabhu. Mahāprabhu instructed them all to chant the holy names.

At that time, a Vaiṣṇava named Kṛṣṇadāsa arrived. He was of the Rājputa caste, a householder, and lived in a village on the bank of the Yamunā River. Kṛṣṇadāsa had taken a bath at Keśī Ghāṭa and on his way to Kālīya-daha, he suddenly saw Mahāprabhu at Imlītalā. Seeing Mahāprabhu's beautiful form and behavior, Kṛṣṇadāsa became overcome by astonishment. He offered his obeisance to Mahāprabhu. Mahāprabhu asked him, "Who are you? Where is your home?" Kṛṣṇadāsa replied, "I am a very lowly householder from the Rājputa caste, and my home is on that side. My desire is to become a servant of the Vaiṣṇavas. However, today I saw a dream; now I am seeing that dream manifest by seeing You." Mahāprabhu bestowed His mercy upon Kṛṣṇadāsa, hugging him. Kṛṣṇadāsa became intoxicated in divine love and danced and chanted "Hari!" He went with Mahāprabhu to Akrūra-tīrtha in the afternoon and got to eat the remnants of Mahāprabhu's meal. In the morning, Kṛṣṇadāsa went with Mahāprabhu, holding Mahāprabhu's water pot. Kṛṣṇadāsa stayed with Mahāprabhu, leaving behind his house, wife, and son.

Vṛndāvana Residents See Mahāprabhu as Kṛṣṇa

People all over Vṛndāvana began to say that Kṛṣṇa had manifested once again in Vṛndāvana. One day, in the morning, many people came from Vṛndāvana to Akrūra-tirtha, causing a huge commotion. When they saw Mahāprabhu, they offered their obeisance to His lotus feet. Mahāprabhu asked, "Where are you coming from?" They replied, "Kṛṣṇa has manifested in the waters of Kālīya-daha. He is dancing on the head of the Kālīya snake and the jewels on the hoods of the snake are shining." There is no doubt that the people saw Him (as Mahāprabhu is Kṛṣṇa). Mahāprabhu laughed and said, "Everything is true." In this way, for three nights, people went to see that sight in the Yamunā and said, "I saw Kṛṣṇa." People went in front of Mahāprabhu and said, "We saw Kṛṣṇa." By Sarasvatī Devī's potency, their words were true, as seeing Mahāprabhu is the same as seeing Kṛṣṇa. However, they thought what they saw in the Yamunā was Kṛṣṇa, accepting that which is false to be true. Balabhadra Bhaṭṭācārya then requested Mahāprabhu, "Please give me the order to go and see Kṛṣṇa!" Mahāprabhu slapped Balabhadra Bhaṭṭācārya and said, "Despite being a *paṇḍita*, you have become a fool by listening to the talks of foolish people. Why will Kṛṣṇa reveal Himself in Kali-yuga? People are fooled by their own misconceptions and are making a commotion. To take that which is not transcendental to be transcendental is craziness. Go home and sit down. You can see 'Kṛṣṇa' tomorrow night."

In the morning, the people came to Mahāprabhu. Mahāprabhu asked them, "Did you see Kṛṣṇa?" They replied, "We saw that in the night there was a boat with a fisherman at Kālīya-daha who had lit a torch with fire." From afar, the people mistook this sight to be Kṛṣṇa dancing on Kālīya. The foolish people thought the boat was Kālīya, the lamp to be jewels, and the fisherman to be Kṛṣṇa! It was true that Kṛṣṇa had come to Vṛndāvana; it was not false that the people saw Kṛṣṇa. However, they saw Kṛṣṇa in one place and an illusion in another, just like when people see a tree without leaves from afar, they mistake it for a man. Mahāprabhu asked, "Where did you see Kṛṣṇa?" They replied, "O *sannyāsī*, You are the walking Nārāyaṇa. You have come to Vṛndāvana in the form of Kṛṣṇa. By seeing you, everyone has become delivered." Mahāprabhu said, "Viṣṇu! Viṣṇu! Do not say that. Never mistake a fallen soul to be Kṛṣṇa! The *sannyāsī* is a tiny fire spark of consciousness. Kṛṣṇa is the posessor of six types of controllership and opulence. Kṛṣṇa is like the sun. The *jīva* (soul) and Kṛṣṇa (Iśvara) are never the same, just like a spark of fire is not the same as the blazing fire itself. Iśvara is always eternal, cognizant and blissful; He is surrounded by the pleasure-giving (*hlādinī*) and cognizance (*saṁvit*) potencies. However, the *jīva* is always surrounded by lack of knowledge (*avidyā*) and is a mine of suffering. The fool who says that the *jīva* and Iśvara are the same is a gross offender and Yamarāja will punish him." One who sees Brahma, Rudra, and so on to be equal to Nārāyaṇa is certainly a *pāṣaṇḍī*, as he is overcome by illusion, thinking the material world and the controller of the material world (Viṣṇu) to be the same.

The people said, "We never see You as a *jīva*. Your form and nature are like that of Kṛṣṇa's. By Your form, we see You as Vrajendra-nandana, whom Your golden complexion has covered. Just as the aroma of musk covered by a cloth cannot be hidden, similarly, You, being the Supreme Lord, cannot be hidden. Your nature cannot be understood, as it is beyond the ability of the intelligence to understand. By seeing You, the whole world becomes mad in divine love for Kṛṣṇa. Women, children, the aged, and sinful outcastes (*caṇḍalās* and *yavanas*) chant the name of Kṛṣṇa just be seeing You once; they dance in an intoxicated manner and deliver the world as *ācāryas*. Leave aside seeing You, one who even hears Your name becomes intoxicated in transcendental love for Kṛṣṇa and delivers the three worlds. Dog-eaters and fallen people become pure deliverers by hearing Your name. Your power is indescribably transcendental. O Supreme Lord, just by hearing, chanting, and remembering Your names, the most fallen (*caṇḍalās* and *yavanas*) become qualified to perform *yajñas*; You are so powerful. What remains impossible for one who can see You? This is Your glory, and it is just Your *taṭastha-lakṣaṇa* quality (that which is understood about You through making comparisons). Your *svarūpa-lakṣaṇa* quality is in being Vrajendra-nandana, and that is how we see You as Kṛṣṇa." All the people pleased Mahāprabhu and they went home in a state of intoxication in transcendental love for Kṛṣṇa.

In this manner, Mahāprabhu stayed for some days in Akrūra-tīrtha. By giving out divine love through the names of Kṛṣṇa, Mahāprabhu delivered the people. The Sanoḍiyā *brāhmaṇa* who was a disciple of Mādhavendra Purī went from house to house giving them the opportunity to serve Mahāprabhu. All the *brāhmaṇas* of Mathurā approached Balabhadra Bhaṭṭācārya, inviting Mahāprabhu to their homes. Ten to twenty invitations would come in a day. Balabhadra Bhaṭṭācārya would only accept one invitation. Many people did not get the opportunity to serve Mahāprabhu, as there were so many invitations being given, and they would approach the Sanoḍiyā *brāhmaṇa* to have their invitations accepted. The Vaidika *brāhmaṇas* of Kānyakubja and Dākṣiṇātya also humbly invited Mahāprabhu. In the morning, they would come to Akrūra-tīrtha, cook, offer the foodstuffs to *śālagrāma-śilā*, and then feed Mahāprabhu.

Departure from Vṛndāvana

One day, Mahāprabhu sat at Akrūra-ghāṭa and thought, "At this *ghāṭa*, Akrūra saw Vaikuṇṭha and the Vrajavāsīs saw Goloka." Thinking this, Mahāprabhu jumped into the water and remained underwater. Kṛṣṇadāsa saw this and cried loudly. Balabhadra Bhaṭṭācārya quickly came and lifted Mahāprabhu out of the water. Balabhadra Bhaṭṭācārya discussed with the *brāhmaṇa* privately, "Today I was present and was able to lift Mahāprabhu out of the water. If He drowns in Vṛndāvana, who will lift Him out? There are always huge crowds of people and the problem of too many invitations for meals and Mahāprabhu is always in ecstasy. It doesn't seem good. It will be auspicious if we take Mahāprabhu out of Vṛndāvana."

The *brāhmaṇa* said, "Take Mahāprabhu to Prayāga. Take Him along the path of the Gaṅgā; then He will be happy. First take Him to Sorokṣetra (the closest access to the Gaṅgā from Mathurā) and have Him bathe there in the Gaṅgā. Take Mahāprabhu along that path. It is now the month of Māgha and if you leave now, then you can take bath in the sacred rivers in Prayāga by Makara-saṅkrānti. Express your sadness to Mahāprabhu and propose taking bath in Prayāga on Makara-saṅkrānti. Tell Him about the happiness along the Gaṅgā path."

Balabhadra Bhaṭṭācārya told Mahāprabhu, "I am unable to tolerate all the crowds and associated issues. Everybody is in a frenzy to invite You for meals. People come in the morning, and if they do not find You, pick my brain to find out Your whereabouts. I will be happy if we can go along the path of the Gaṅgā. If we leave now, we will be able to reach Prayāga by Makara-saṅkrānti and take bath in the Gaṅgā there. My life is becoming very difficult, and I am unable to tolerate it. However, whatever You decide, I shall follow." Although Mahāprabhu did not want to leave Vṛndāvana, Mahāprabhu spoke sweet words to satisfy the desires of His devotee. Mahāprabhu said, "You brought Me here and showed Me Vṛndāvana. I will not be able to repay this debt to you. I shall do whatever you desire. I shall go wherever you take Me."

In the morning, Mahāprabhu took a bath and became overwhelmed in divine love, knowing that He would be leaving Vṛndāvana. Externally Mahāprabhu showed no changes, but His mind was overcome by ecstatic love. Balabhadra Bhaṭṭācārya said, "Come on. Let's go to Mahāvana." He took Mahāprabhu on the boat to cross the Yamunā. The Rājputa Kṛṣṇadāsa and Sanoḍiyā *brāhmaṇa* knew the path along the Gaṅgā very well. In this way, Mahāprabhu left Vṛndāvana for Prayāga.

Discussions with Rūpa Gosvāmī

Later, when Mahāprabhu was returning from Vṛndāvana, He met Rūpa Gosvāmī in Prayāga and Sanātana Gosvāmī in Vārāṇasī and taught them both various aspects of devotional philosophy and practice. Mahāprabhu instructed Rūpa and Sanātana to go to Vṛndāvana to recover the lost holy places where Kṛṣṇa performed pastimes, to write books on devotional service, and to establish temples where deity forms of Śrī Śrī Rādhā Kṛṣṇa could be worshiped. These instructions were very significant because, through Rūpa and Sanātana, Mahāprabhu established the foundations of the Vaiṣṇava tradition.

Rūpa and Sanātana had been contemplating how to release themselves from government service and join Śrī Chaitanya Mahāprabhu. Rūpa donated his wealth by dividing it amongst the Vaiṣṇavas, *brāhmaṇas*, and family relatives. He had sent some servants to Jagannātha Purī to find out when Mahāprabhu would start for Vṛndāvana and, accordingly, he and his brother Anupama left toward the north to reach the holy city of Prayāga (currently known as Prayāga-rāja). It was there that Rūpa Gosvāmī finally got the opportunity to sit for ten days with Mahāprabhu on the banks of the Gaṅgā River at the Daśa-aśvamedha Ghāṭa and learn the confidential secrets of devotion.

Mahāprabhu instructed Rūpa Gosvāmī on *abhidheya*, the process of devotion, and empowered him with devotional potency. Mahāprabhu also instructed Rūpa on the conclusions that He had heard from the mouth of Rāmānanda Rāya in South India. Mahāprabhu explained to Rūpa Gosvāmī that He would be instructing him on just a drop of the deep ocean of devotional mellows (*bhakti-rasāmṛta-sindhu*). Mahāprabhu explained as follows: The living entity (*jīva*) is one ten-thousandth the size of the tip of a strand of hair. Amongst the moving and non-moving living entities, the humans are a small minority. Amongst those, most are fallen. Of those that believe in the Vedas, half of them just follow in name only. Amongst the Vedic practitioners, most are committed to fruitive activities. Amongst ten million such practitioners, one who follows the pursuit of spiritual knowledge is the best. Amongst ten million such seekers of spiritual knowledge, one may be considered liberated. Amongst ten million such liberated persons, one devotee of Kṛṣṇa is very rare.

The devotees of Kṛṣṇa are peaceful, as they are free from desiring material sense enjoyment, liberation, mystic powers, and material things. The living entity wanders throughout the universe, and out of good fortune attains the seed of devotion. That seed is to be sown and watered by the gardener with the water of hearing and chanting about Kṛṣṇa. Eventually the creeper of devotion grows, going past the Virajā, Brahmaloka, and the Paravyoma, and eventually reaches Goloka Vṛndāvana, where it reaches the wish-fulfilling lotus feet of Śrī Kṛṣṇa. The fruit of divine love grows from this creeper and is constantly watered by the water of hearing and chanting. However, if offenses are committed against Vaiṣṇavas, which are like a mad elephant, then the creeper of devotion gets uprooted and destroyed. The spiritual practitioner must protect against the mad elephant of offense. In addition, the weeds of desiring material sense enjoyment, liberation, illicit activities, deception, violence of any sort, greed, worship, position, etc., also grow during the watering process and must be uprooted. Otherwise, they will stifle the growth of the main creeper of devotion. When the fruit of transcendental love ripens, the gardener relishes it and attains the wish-fulfilling tree of Kṛṣṇa and serves Kṛṣṇa in bliss while relishing the nectar of divine love. This divine love is the ultimate goal of life and makes the other four goals of life (material sense enjoyment, religiosity, wealth, and liberation) seem insignificant.

Divine love arises from pure devotion which is free from fruitive activities, the pursuit of knowledge, as well as desires and worship unrelated to Kṛṣṇa. When the living entity is free from all material designations and engages the senses in the service of Hṛṣīkeśa, that is known as devotion (*bhakti*). The practice of devotion leads to attachment which, when thickened, becomes known as divine love. This love thickens into deeper and deeper stages of affection, just as the juice of sugarcane is sweeter and sweeter as the sugar gets more and more condensed. Further, there are five main sentiments through which one develops a relationship with Kṛṣṇa: the moods of neutrality, servitude, friendship, parenthood, and conjugal love. There are also transient moods, which include laughter, amazement, valor, compassion, anger, ghastliness, and fear. The Yogendras and the Sanaka brothers are in the mood of neutrality. The servants are in the mood of servitude. Śrīdāmā, Bhīma, and Arjuna are in the mood of friendship. The mothers, fathers, and elders are in the mood of parenthood. The Vraja *gopis* are in the mood of conjugal love.

There are two types of attachment to Kṛṣṇa: one that is mixed with attention given to Kṛṣṇa's controllership, and one that is pure attachment that neglects even the godliness of God. This latter type is present in Gokula, while the love mixed with awe is present in Mathurā and in Dvārakā and has some inhibition present within it. For example, when Vasudeva and Devakī saw Kṛṣṇa, they had some inhibition and fear. Similarly, when Arjuna saw the universal form of Kṛṣṇa, he became fearful and then apologized for how he used to behave so freely with Kṛṣṇa. When Kṛṣṇa joked with Rukmiṇī, Rukmiṇī would feel scared that Kṛṣṇa would leave her. However, other devotees, despite knowing the godliness of Kṛṣṇa, do not give importance to it and rather maintain the mellow of their specific relationship with Kṛṣṇa. For instance, Śrīdāmā sees Kṛṣṇa purely as His friend, and Śrī Rādhā knows how Kṛṣṇa is totally under Her influence.

The two qualities of those in the mood of neutrality is fixedness in Kṛṣṇa and the renunciation of material desire. Those with that mood do not have any feeling of possession over Kṛṣṇa; they see Him as the *param-brahma* and *paramātma*. Those in the mood of servitude see Kṛṣṇa as God and have much respect for Him. Thus, they feel that they can give Him happiness by serving Him. Those in the mood of friendship serve Kṛṣṇa, make Kṛṣṇa serve them, and have deep intimacy with Kṛṣṇa. Being free from inhibition and fearful respect, they feel much possessiveness of Kṛṣṇa. Those in the mood of parenthood scold and punish Kṛṣṇa, see themselves as the protector of Kṛṣṇa, and see Kṛṣṇa as the one who needs protection.

Kṛṣṇa drowns Himself in this nectar of bliss, along with His devotees. He is subordinate to the devotion of His devotees. Those in the mood of conjugal love are fixed in their devotion to Kṛṣṇa and serve Him copiously. They have no inhibition in their love and have great possessiveness for Kṛṣṇa with a desire to serve Him. They give their very bodies in the service of Kṛṣṇa. Each progressive mood has the qualities of the preceding mood and relationship with Kṛṣṇa. This is just a small description of the mellows of devotion. By continuously thinking of Kṛṣṇa, He manifests within; by His mercy, even an ignorant person can traverse the ocean of devotional mellows.

After illuminating these topics, Mahāprabhu instructed Rūpa Gosvāmī to go to Vṛndāvana, but Rūpa Gosvāmī could not tolerate the pangs of separation. However, Mahāprabhu said that Rūpa Gosvāmī should go to Vṛndāvana and then meet with Him in Jagannātha Purī by traveling from Vṛndāvana through Bengal. Mahāprabhu embraced Rūpa Gosvāmī and then left by boat. Rūpa Gosvāmī fainted right there.

Talks with Sanātana Gosvāmī

Thereafter, Mahāprabhu reached Vārāṇasī and began staying in the house of Candraśekhara Ācārya. Meanwhile, Sanātana Gosvāmī had stopped working for the Muslim government upon the pretext that he was unwell. In actuality, he was studying the *Śrīmad-Bhāgavatam* with scholars at his home. The Muslim officers came to check on him one day and saw that he was studying the *Śrīmad-Bhāgavatam*. Thus, they put him in jail. While Sanātana Gosvāmī was in jail, Rūpa Gosvāmī sent him a letter saying that Mahāprabhu had reached Mathurā. Sanātana Gosvāmī began speaking very sweet words to the jailkeeper and persuaded the jailkeeper to release him by enticing him with seven thousand gold coins. The gatekeeper released Sanātana Gosvāmī. Along with his servant, Īśāna, Sanātana Gosvāmī reached Pātaḍā Mountain. Once there, he requested some people to help him cross the mountain. However, these people were bandits and they had used some astrological calculations to find out that there were eight gold coins with Sanātana and Īśāna. They were exceedingly cordial with Sanātana Gosvāmī, offering him food and so on, which raised a doubt in Sanātana Gosvāmī's mind. Sanātana Gosvāmī asked Īśāna if he was carrying any money and found out that he had seven gold coins with him. The chief bandit was planning to kill Sanātana Gosvāmī to get the money. Sanātana Gosvāmī told Īśāna to give the money to the bandit, and the person helped them cross over the mountain. Thereafter, Sanātana Gosvāmī understood that Īśāna must have kept some more money with him and Īśāna admitted that he had another gold coin with him. Thus, understanding all this to be an unwanted predicament, Sanātana Gosvāmī sent Īśāna back home and started traveling on his own.

On the way, Śrīkānta, who was Sanātana Gosvāmī's brother-in-law, saw Sanātana Gosvāmī and heard about all that had taken place. He helped Sanātana Gosvāmī cross the Gaṅgā. Śrīkānta also gave him a type of shawl (*bhoṭa-kambala*). Sanātana Gosvāmī finally reached Vārāṇasī and was standing outside the house of Candraśekhara. Mahāprabhu told Candraśekhara to call him in, but Candraśekhara just thought that Sanātana was a Muslim mendicant due to his ragged condition after the long travel. Mahāprabhu came out and hugged Sanātana and told him to change his clothes. Sanātana Gosvāmī took the clothes that were given to him by Tapana Miśra and made a *kaupīna* and outer covering with the cloth. Sanātana Gosvāmī also let go of his *bhoṭa-kambala* at the bank of the Gaṅgā and took a torn piece of cloth for covering his upper body known as a *kanṭha*. Seeing this mood of renunciation in Sanātana Gosvāmī, Mahāprabhu became very happy.

Thereafter, Mahāprabhu began instructing Sanātana Gosvāmī on the teachings of pure devotion (*śuddha-bhakti*) regarding establishing one's eternal relationship with the Supreme Lord (*sambandha*), practicing devotion (*abhidheya*), and attaining the goal of divine love (*prayojana*). Śrīla Sanātana Gosvāmīpāda offered his obeisance to Śrīman Mahāprabhu's lotus feet and asked, "O Master! Who am I? Why am I forced to be burned by the threefold miseries of material existence (*tri-tāpa*) caused by the body and mind (*ādhyātmika*), by other living entities (*ādhibhautika*), and by the natural calamities caused by the higher living entities (*ādhidaivika*)? How will I be able to achieve true auspiciousness? I do not know how to inquire about the spiritual practice and the goal of spiritual practice (*sādhya-sādhana-tattva*). Please mercifully instruct me on everything that I should know and everything that I should do."

Mahāprabhu explained that regarding the constitutional position of the living entity, the soul (*jīva*) is constitutionally the eternal servant of Kṛṣṇa (*nitya-dāsa*). The *jīva* is the *taṭasthā* potency of Kṛṣṇa. The *jīva* is similar to Kṛṣṇa and is manifested in simultaneous oneness and difference from Kṛṣṇa (*bhedābheda prakāśa*). This description, in totality, is known as the relationship between the *jīva* and Kṛṣṇa, or, in other words, it is known as *sambandha*. Kṛṣṇa has three energies known as the potency of knowledge (*cit-śakti*), the potency of the living entity (*jīva-śakti*), and the potency of illusion (*māyā-śakti*). Since the living entities have forgotten Kṛṣṇa, Kṛṣṇa has made the scriptures through which the living entity can be reminded of Him. The Supreme Lord has three aspects: the effulgent Brahman, the localized supersoul (Paramātmā), and the Lord full in all His opulences, known as Bhagavān. Mahāprabhu went on to explain all the various forms of Kṛṣṇa such as Vaibhava, Prābhava, Puruṣāvatāra, Manvantarāvatāra, Guṇāvatāra, Śaktyāveśāvatāra, and so on. Mahāprabhu also described the various pastimes of Kṛṣṇa according to Kṛṣṇa's ages. Mahāprabhu explained about the sixty-four types of *sādhana-bhakti*, which is devotion performed according to rules and regulations. Finally, Mahāprabhu explained *rāgānuga-bhakti*, wherein the living entity develops intense love for Kṛṣṇa.

A living entity practicing *rāgānuga-bhakti* desires to follow in the footsteps of one of the residents of Vṛndāvana according to five main devotional mellows, as previously explained to Rūpa Gosvāmī. Mahāprabhu explained the various types of *bhāva* and *prema* and their symptoms. He explained the sixty-four qualities of Kṛṣṇa and the twenty-five qualities of Śrī Rādhā. Then Mahāprabhu described the sixty-one explanations of the Śrīmad-*Bhāgavatam* verse beginning *ātmārāmāś ca munayo*. One of the meanings of this verse is that even the liberated persons who are self-satisfied are attracted to the pastimes of Lord Kṛṣṇa and devotion to Him.

After Rūpa Gosvāmī reached Vṛndāvana, he met Subuddhi Rāya at Dhruva Ghāṭa on the banks of the Yamunā River. Subuddhi Rāya explained about what had happened to him in Bengal. Subuddhi Rāya used to be a prestigious landowner and he had engaged Saiyad Hussein Khān in digging a lake. However, having found some fault in the job, Subuddhi Rāya whipped Hussein Khān. Later, when Hussein Khān became the Nawab of the Muslim leadership in Bengal, he punished Subuddhi Rāya, being influenced by his own wife. When she saw the marks from the whip on her husband's back, his wife wanted Hussein to kill Subuddhi Rāya or to remove his high caste status. Hussein Khān was very perplexed because he felt that Subuddhi Rāya was like his father from their earlier relationship; however, his wife wanted Subuddhi to be killed. Finally, Hussein Khān had the water from a Muslim's water pot thrown on Subuddhi Rāya's face. This caused his high caste status to be destroyed. Upon the pretext of losing his caste, Subuddhi Rāya left for Vārāṇasī. Various *paṇḍitas* recommended to him that he drink burning hot ghee and then take a new birth. Others said that such a difficult repentance was not necessary for the relatively small defect of having lost one's caste.

When Mahāprabhu came to Vārāṇasī, Subuddhi Rāya met Him and was instructed by Mahāprabhu to go to Vṛndāvana and constantly chant the names of Kṛṣṇa. Mahāprabhu explained that by chanting a semblance of the holy names (*nāmābhāsa*), all sins would be destroyed. Then, by chanting another name of Kṛṣṇa, one will reach the lotus feet of Kṛṣṇa. By chanting the third name, one reaches a place in the spiritual world of Kṛṣṇa. This is the greatest repentance for the most sinful people. Having received this instruction, Subuddhi Rāya went to Vṛndāvana. This extreme power of the holy names was explained in this way by Mahāprabhu.

Part IV
Final Years

Ecstatic Pastimes in Jagannātha Purī

After touring the pilgrimage places in northern India—Vṛndāvana, Mathurā, Prayāga, Vārāṇasī—Mahāprabhu returned to Purī in around 1515 and remained there until His departure from this world in 1533. King Pratāparudra's spiritual master, Kāśī Miśra, had a cottage built on his property for Mahāprabhu. This cottage was known as the Gambhīrā. Mahāprabhu's interest in external matters diminished day by day. Close devotees like Svarūpa Dāmodara, Rāmānanda Rāya, and Parāmānanda Purī remained with Him. Nevertheless, in the intensity of His absorption in the mood of Śrīmatī Rādhārāṇī, He became progressively unconscious of the world around Him. Extraordinary ecstatic symptoms manifested on Mahāprabhu's body. Sometimes in a state of divine madness, He would run to the entrance of the Jagannātha temple and fall unconscious.

During Mahāprabhu's stay in Purī, a very beautiful boy, the son of a young *brāhmaṇa* widow, used to come daily to meet Mahāprabhu. Mahāprabhu loved the boy and would express His affection. The boy was also very much attached to Mahāprabhu and could not live without seeing Him. Dāmodara Paṇḍita was a great scholar. He could not tolerate that this boy, the son of a widow, was coming to see Mahāprabhu. He felt that people would speak ill of Mahāprabhu if they came to know that He was showing affection to the son of a young widow. Mahāprabhu, in response, said that there was nobody more intimate to Him than Dāmodara Paṇḍita. Thereafter, Mahāprabhu told Dāmodara Paṇḍita to go to Śacī Devī to take care of her. He told Dāmodara Paṇḍita to tell her that He comes and takes *prasāda* in her home from time to time. In this way, Dāmodara Paṇḍita took Jagannātha's *mahāprasāda* and went to Navadvīpa.

One day, a resident of Sylhet, Bangladesh, named Pradyumna Miśra came to Jagannātha Purī to hear the glories of Lord Hari from Śrī Chaitanya Mahāprabhu. Mahāprabhu expressed His ignorance of knowledge about Lord Kṛṣṇa and sent Pradyumna to Rāya Rāmānanda to learn from him instead. When Pradyumna Miśra went to Rāya Rāmānanda, he saw that Rāya Rāmānanda was teaching the young dancing Jagannātha temple girls how to act out the drama that he had composed, named *Jagannātha Vallabha Nāṭakam*. Rāya Rāmānanda was totally absorbed in the mood of being a maidservant and was personally teaching the girls how to sing and dance for Lord Jagannātha.

After a long time of serving and teaching the girls, Rāya Rāmānanda came and saw that Pradyumna Miśra was waiting to meet him. Rāya Rāmānanda immediately apologized for making him wait and then asked him how he could serve him. Pradyumna Miśra replied by explaining how he had come just to see Rāya Rāmānanda. Thereafter, Pradyumna Miśra went back to Mahāprabhu and explained what had happened. Mahāprabhu, out of humility, explained how Rāya Rāmānanda was a perfected spiritual personality who was totally untouched by the urges of the human body; he was completely situated in the platform of transcendence. Mahāprabhu instructed Pradyumna Miśra to go back to Rāya Rāmānanda and tell him that he was sent by Mahāprabhu.

Pradyumna Miśra went back to Rāya Rāmānanda and explained that Mahāprabhu had sent him to hear about Lord Kṛṣṇa. Rāya Rāmānanda became overwhelmed when he heard that Mahāprabhu had sent Pradyumna Miśra to him. Thereafter, he started explaining the topics of devotion to Kṛṣṇa filled with the mellows of divine love. In this way, both Pradyumna Miśra and Rāya Rāmānanda became overwhelmed in the ocean of spiritual emotion for Kṛṣṇa. After a very long time, Pradyumna Miśra took his leave and went back to Mahāprabhu. He explained how Rāya Rāmānanda was not somebody of the material world but rather a completely spiritual personality. In this way, Mahāprabhu broadcast the glories of Rāya Rāmānanda by making a renounced person, namely Pradyumna Miśra, go and listen from

Rāya Rāmānanda, who was externally a *gṛhastha*. Rāya Rāmānanda may have been a *gṛhastha* externally, but he was transcendental to all bodily urges and was situated in the highest states of divine love for Kṛṣṇa.

One day, Mahāprabhu took all the devotees to Lord Jagannātha's temple and began a grand congregational chanting of the holy names. There were seven groups, and they all began singing and dancing. Mahāprabhu manifested His divine potency and became present in all seven groups. All the residents of Purī came to see this divine *saṅkīrtana* going on in the Jagannātha temple. The king along with his associates also came to witness this ecstatic event. Mahāprabhu then began to dance in the middle of all seven groups. He was completely overwhelmed in ecstasy. Mahāprabhu began singing an Odia song, *Jagamohana-pari-muṇḍa yau*, and fainted. Everyone was raising their hands, saying "Haribol!" and floating in bliss. Mahāprabhu's body exhibited all the symptoms of ecstasy. He was saying, "*Jaja, gaga, pari, mumu.*" Nityānanda Prabhu devised a way to make the *kīrtana* gradually come to an end so that Mahāprabhu would be saved from all the physical ecstasies. Mahāprabhu and the devotees then all honored *prasāda* and the devotees went to their respective places of residence.

Mahāprabhu was very tired and lay down right at the doorway of His room, called the Gambhīrā. Govinda, Mahāprabhu's servant, came to massage Mahāprabhu's lotus feet and requested Him to please move His body completely inside the room. However, Mahāprabhu said that He was too tired and could not move even one limb of His body. Mahāprabhu fell asleep right in the middle of the doorway. Govinda put his upper garment over Mahāprabhu, crossed over His body, then began massaging Mahāprabhu's lotus feet. Govinda did not exit the room while Mahāprabhu was sleeping. When Mahāprabhu woke up, He saw Govinda sitting inside the room and asked him why he was still sitting there and had not gone to take *prasāda*. Govinda said, "You were sleeping at the door so I couldn't exit." Mahāprabhu asked, "How did you enter the room? Why couldn't you exit in the same way to go and take *prasāda*?" Govinda replied, "I don't mind even if I must commit ten million offenses for the purpose of serving You. However, for my own self, I am afraid to even commit a semblance of an offense." These are all the very subtle secrets of the devotional scriptures. By Chaitanya Mahāprabhu's mercy, one can understand all these topics.

Sometimes Mahāprabhu would lose Himself in the sand dunes on the beach, running toward them with the speed of the wind, taking them to be Govardhana Hill in Vṛndāvana. Sometimes He would dive into the ocean, thinking it was the Yamunā River where Kṛṣṇa had His pastimes. One full-moon night, Mahāprabhu was walking with His devotees from one flower garden to another, singing the verses from the *Bhāgavatam* commemorating the *rāsa-līlā*. When they came to the garden known as Āiṭoṭā, Mahāprabhu caught a glimpse of the ocean, with the silver effulgence of the moon reflected on its dancing waves. Mahāprabhu's memory of the Yamunā was enkindled and He ran toward the sea as fast as He was able and jumped into the water. While He was in a trance-like state, seeing Himself as a servant of the *gopīs* participating in Kṛṣṇa's water games in the Yamunā, the outgoing tide pulled His body away from the shore and farther east in the direction of Koṇārka.

None of the other devotees had been able to see where Mahāprabhu had fallen into the water. Svarūpa Dāmodara and the others began to search for Him everywhere along the shore. Unable to find him anywhere, they brokenheartedly concluded that He had drowned and would never be seen again. As they were lamenting the loss of Mahāprabhu, Svarūpa Dāmodara saw a fisherman walking on the beach, ecstatically calling out the names of Kṛṣṇa. Suspecting that there was some connection, Svarūpa Dāmodara asked the fisherman the reason for his ecstatic state. The fisherman answered that he had been fishing at night when he had felt something large tugging on his net. Upon pulling it up, he had found what he thought was a dead body, but the moment he touched it, divine ecstasy entered his own body like an electric current. He could not understand what had happened and concluded he had been caught by a supernatural being or ghost. After hearing this account from the fisherman, everyone immediately understood that he was talking about Mahāprabhu and, after reassuring him, insisted on being led to Mahāprabhu.

The devotees changed Mahāprabhu into dry clothes. As He returned to a state of semi-awareness, He told them about the visions He had seen: "I went to Vṛndāvana and saw Kṛṣṇa there with the *gopīs*, splashing each other and playing hide-and-seek in the waters of the Yamunā. I stood on the shore with the other cowherd girls and watched them play."

One day, Mahāprabhu was on his way to the ocean. On the way, He saw a sand dune known as Caṭaka Parvata and suddenly became overwhelmed in ecstasy, thinking it to be Govardhana Hill. He ran as fast as the wind, repeating a verse from the *Śrīmad-Bhāgavatam* which describes that Govardhana is the best of devotees. All the devotees followed Mahāprabhu. Mahāprabhu first ran as fast as the wind and then suddenly stopped like a pillar. Each of His pores were swelling, with hairs standing on end like a *campaka* flower. His words were not understandable. Tears were flowing from His eyes and the streams of tears were joining with the ocean, as if they were the Yamunā and Gaṅgā rivers. His body trembled like waves in the ocean. Mahāprabhu fell to the ground and Govinda went near Him. Govinda sprinkled water on Mahāprabhu's whole body and then fanned Him with His outer cloth. Svarūpa Dāmodara and other devotees came and saw Mahāprabhu and began to weep. They wiped His body with cool water and sang *kīrtana*, while chanting, "Haribol."

Suddenly, Mahāprabhu arose and started going here and there, not being able to find that what He was looking for. He was in a half-awakened consciousness and started saying to Svarūpa Dāmodara, "Who brought me here from Govardhana? I attained Kṛṣṇa's pastimes but am now unable to see these pastimes. Today, I went to Govardhana from here. I saw that Kṛṣṇa climbed on top of Govardhana while grazing the cows. He was grazing the cows all over Vṛndāvana. Hearing Kṛṣṇa's flute, Rādhā Ṭhākurānī came along with all Her *sakhīs*. Kṛṣṇa entered a cave along with Rādhārāṇī. The *sakhīs* told Me to pick some flowers. From there, you have brought Me here. Why did you bring Me here to give Me unnecessary suffering? I was witnessing Kṛṣṇa's pastimes but now am unable to see them!" Saying this, Mahāprabhu started crying and all the Vaiṣṇavas also started crying. Then, Mahāprabhu gained full external consciousness and could see Purī and Bhāratī. The devotees all hugged Mahāprabhu. Mahāprabhu asked them, "Why did you come so far?" They replied, "To see Your dancing." Mahāprabhu felt shy. Then, all the devotees along with Mahāprabhu went to the ocean and bathed. Mahāprabhu went back to His room and all the devotees took *mahāprāsada* there.

Chaitanya's Relationship with Haridāsa Ṭhākura

Haridāsa Ṭhākura was born in a Muslim family in Jessore, Bangladesh. However, he was a devotee of Lord Hari from his childhood and moved to Benapole as a youth after being kicked out by the Muslims. There, he lived alone chanting the holy names. He used to chant three hundred thousand names every day. Despite being tested many times by various forces, he never gave up chanting. He was constantly fixed on chanting the holy names. Advaita Ācārya highly respected Haridāsa Ṭhākura. Towards the end of his life, Haridāsa Ṭhākura was given a secluded place by Mahāprabhu in Jagannātha Purī for chanting the holy names. This place is currently called Siddha-bakula.

While in Jagannātha Purī, Mahāprabhu would visit Haridāsa Ṭhākura every day. Towards the very end of his life, Haridāsa Ṭhākura was unable to complete his daily quota of holy names. At that time, Mahāprabhu came to see him and told him not to worry about completing chanting all his prescribed number of names every day. Haridāsa Ṭhākura explained how he was not worried about his body, but that his mind was afflicted due to being unable to complete all the names. Haridāsa Ṭhākura begged for Mahāprabhu to be present at the time when he would leave his body. Finally, on his last day, Haridāsa Ṭhākura had the good fortune of seeing Mahāprabhu. He placed his two bee-like eyes on the lotus-like face of Mahāprabhu, held Mahāprabhu's feet to his chest, and said, "Śrī Kṛṣṇa Chaitanya," as he left his body. While chanting the holy names, Mahāprabhu carried Haridāsa Ṭhākura's body and danced in ecstatic bliss. He personally bathed Haridāsa Ṭhākura's body in the Purī ocean and then placed Haridāsa Ṭhākura's body in *samādhi*, along with various articles that had been used in Lord Jagannātha's service, such as Jagannātha's cloth and the rope from the *ratha-yātrā*. Mahāprabhu organized a huge festival and arranged for *mahāprāsadā* to be brought from Lord Jagannātha's temple. Mahāprabhu was far beyond all caste discrimination. He was the personification of divine love. Mahāprabhu never discriminated between Hindus or Muslims or various castes and creeds—He loves all devotees!

Jagadānanda Paṇḍita and Mahāprabhu

Mahāprabhu had sent Jagadānanda Paṇḍita from Purī to Śacī Mātā. He gave Śacī Mātā Jagannātha's cloth and offered obeisance on behalf of Mahāprabhu. Jagadānanda explained that while Mahāprabhu would sometimes come and take *prasāda* at Śacī Mātā's, she felt that it was all just a dream. In this way, Jagadānanda told Śacī Mātā the pastimes of Chaitanya Mahāprabhu day and night. Thereafter, to whomever's house Jagadānanda went to in Nadia, he would discuss the pastimes of Mahāprabhu. When everyone met and spoke with Jagadānanada Paṇḍita, they felt as if they directly were receiving Mahāprabhu in their homes.

Jagadānanda Paṇḍita prepared a very fragrant sandalwood oil for Mahāprabhu and brought it all the way back to Jagannātha Purī. There, he requested Govinda to apply it on Mahāprabhu's head. However, Mahāprabhu said that it was inappropriate for *sannyāsīs* to use it and instructed that the oil be sent to light the lamps in Lord Jagannātha's temple. Govinda told Jagadānanda and Jagadānanda remained silent. After ten days, Govinda told Mahāprabhu again that Jagadānanda wanted the oil to be used for Mahāprabhu. This time, Mahāprabhu became a bit irritated and said, "Am I a *sannyāsī* who roams around with women (*dārī-sannyāsī*)?" Hearing this, Govinda became quiet. In the morning, Jagadānanda went to Mahāprabhu. Mahāprabhu expressed how He could not use the oil as a *sannyāsī* and that it should be used for the lamps in Jagannātha's temple. Jagadānanda replied, "Who told You this lie? I never brought any oil from Bengal (Gauḍa)." After speaking those words, Jagadānanda took the whole pot of oil and threw it in the courtyard in front of Mahāprabhu, where it broke. From there, Jagadānanda went to his room, locked the door, and slept. He did not eat for two days. On the third day after this event, Mahāprabhu went to Jagadānanda's room and said, "Wake up, Paṇḍita. Today, you shall cook for Me and feed Me. I will come in the afternoon. Now I am going to see Lord Jagannātha." Jagadānanda arose, bathed, and cooked many delectable items for Mahāprabhu. Mahāprabhu came and honored the delicious *prasāda*. Every time He thought to get up, Jagadānanda Paṇḍita would bring another item. However, Mahāprabhu did not say anything in fear that He would upset Jagadānanda, and Jagadānanda would again fast and not eat anything. In this way, Mahāprabhu and Jagadānanda shared loving pastimes.

Honoring the Remnants of the Vaiṣṇavas

bhakta-pada-dhūli āra bhakta-pada-jala
bhakta-bhukta-avaśeṣa, — tina mahā-bala
ei tina-sevā haite kṛṣṇa-premā haya
punaḥ punaḥ sarva-śāstre phukāriyā kaya
(*Caitanya-caritāmṛta, Antya-līlā* 16.60-61)

"The dust of the lotus feet of the devotees, the water that has washed the feet of the pure devotees, and the remnants of the *prasāda* honored by the devotees are extremely powerful. By serving these three, divine love for Kṛṣṇa arises. This has been said in the scriptures again and again."

All the devotees came to Jagannātha Purī from Nadia. At that time, Kālidāsa, who was Raghunātha dāsa Gosvāmī's uncle, also came. He was a great devotee who knew nothing other than the name of Kṛṣṇa. He used to bring nice presents for all the *brāhmaṇa* Vaiṣṇavas and then honor their remnants at the end of their meal. If they wouldn't give him their remnants, then he would hide, wait for the devotees to throw out their remnants, and then eat the remnants. He would even give low-caste people gifts and then wait for their remnants. Once, Kālidāsa went to a low-caste person named Jhaḍu Ṭhākura, gave him mangoes, and offered him obeisance. Kālidāsa then offered his obeisance to Jhaḍu Ṭhākura's wife. Jhaḍu Ṭhākura said, "I am from a low caste, and you are an exalted guest. How can I serve you? I shall arrange for you to have rice in a *brāhmaṇa's* house. Please have *prasāda* there; then I shall be able to live." Kālidāsa said, "O Ṭhākura, have mercy on me. I came to see you and by seeing you, I have become purified. I am fortunate and my life is perfected. I have one desire. Please give me the dust from your lotus feet. Please place your feet on my head."

Jhaḍu Ṭhākura said, "You should not speak like this. I am from a low caste. You are a great personality from a high caste." Kālidāsa spoke a verse from the *Bhāgavata* where someone says that he considers a dog-eater who has offered his mind, words, activites, wealth, and very life to the lotus feet of Acyuta to be more elevated than a *brāhmaṇa* who is repulsive to the lotus feet of Acyuta despite possessing all twelve good qualities. This is because that dog-eater can purify his whole family, whereas a *brāhmaṇa* who is repulsive to Acyuta's lotus feet cannot purify even himself, what to speak of his family. He also described that a dog-eater who chants the names of Hari is purified to the level of a *brāhmaṇa* who performs moon sacrifices. After hearing this, Jhaḍu Ṭhākura said, "This is the truth of the scriptures. He who has devotion to Kṛṣṇa is the topmost. I am from a low caste, and I have no devotion to Kṛṣṇa. Your statements apply to others. I do not have such potency." Thereafter Kālidāsa offered his obeisance and asked for permission to leave. Jhaḍu Ṭhākura followed him to the exit and then went back inside. Kālidāsa took the dust from the footprint of Jhaḍu Ṭhākura on the ground and smeared it all over his body. Jhaḍu Ṭhākura then offered the mangoes to Kṛṣṇa in his mind. He and his wife ate the mangoes and sucked on the seeds. After they finished eating the mangoes, he threw out the seeds and skin in the waste area. Kālidāsa was waiting outside and when he saw the remnants, he went and started sucking on the mango seed. In this way, Kālidāsa became ecstatic in divine love. Kālidāsa used to take the remnants of all the Vaiṣṇavas of Bengal.

Mahāprabhu would wash His feet near the Siṁha-dvāra of Lord Jagannātha's temple every day before entering to see the Lord. He had told His servant, Govinda, not to let anyone drink the water that had washed His feet. One day, when Mahāprabhu was washing His feet, Kālidāsa went there and put out his hands with his palms facing upwards. He drank three handfuls of the water which was falling from Mahāprabhu's feet. After the three handfuls, Mahāprabhu told Kālidāsa to stop, saying, "Don't drink anymore. I have fulfilled your desire in this way." Mahāprabhu knew the devotion of His devotee and thus had mercy on Kālidāsa. This mercy if rare even for the gods. Thereafter, Mahāprabhu offered His prayers to Nṛsiṁhadeva and then to Lord Jagannātha. He then returned home, performed His afternoon prayers, and had *prasāda*. Kālidāsa was waiting at the door and signaled to Govinda of his desire. After Mahāprabhu finished having his *prasāda*, Govinda gave the remnants of Mahāprabhu to Kālidāsa.

Mahāprabhu's Final Pastimes

Every year, Chaitanya Mahāprabhu sent someone to Bengal to bring a reassuring message to Mother Śacī, the incarnation of motherly love. One year He sent Jagadānanda Paṇḍita, who not only went with a message from Mahāprabhu, but on Paramānanda Purī's request, also brought with him a piece of Mahāprabhu's cloth and some sanctified food from the Jagannātha deity. When Jagadānanda went to Bengal, he also visited Navadvīpa and Śāntipura before returning to Purī. During this time, Advaita Prabhu gave Mahāprabhu a message in the form of a riddle. The message was:

bāulake kahiha loka ha-ila bāula
bāulake kahiha hāṭe nā bikāya cāula
bāulake kahiha kāje nāhika āula
bāulake kahiha ihā kahiyāche bāula

(*Caitanya-caritāmṛta, Āntya-līlā* 19.20-21)

> "Tell that crazy man everyone's gone crazy. Tell that crazy man no one's selling rice in the market. Tell that crazy man there's no more use for crazies like him. Tell that crazy man that the crazy man said this."

Nobody could understand what Advaita Ācārya meant by this riddle. There are still many different interpretations of the verse, but it is generally understood to mean: "Everyone has gone crazy with love for Kṛṣṇa, so the market for the holy names has become saturated. There is thus no more need for Mahāprabhu to remain in the world to spread the religious practice of the age." On hearing the message, Mahāprabhu simply said, "So be it." In other words, He agreed to fulfill Advaita's request. This message signaled the beginning of the last chapter of Mahāprabhu's life in this world. For so long He had been cultivating Rādhārāṇī's mood; now He lost Himself in it completely.

Mahāprabhu's divine madness continued to grow stronger and stronger. One night He rubbed His cheek against the wall of the Gambhīrā, trying to get out to find Kṛṣṇa. Svarūpa Dāmodara and Rāmānanda sang the songs of Caṇḍīdāsa, Vidyāpati, and Jayadeva to try to bring Him a little peace of mind. Overall, the last twelve years of Mahāprabhu's life passed in this way. There was barely any difference between His waking and sleeping state.

Most of Mahāprabhu's biographers—Murāri Gupta, Kavi Karṇapūra, Vṛndāvana dāsa, and Kṛṣṇadāsa Kavirāja—have written nothing about His disappearance. Only Locana dāsa writes: "On the third watch on a

Sunday, Mahāprabhu disappeared into Lord Jagannātha's body." (*Caitanya-maṅgala*) According to this account, Mahāprabhu embraced the deity of Lord Jagannātha and disappeared into His body in the mid-afternoon one Sunday at the Guṇḍicā temple. Śrīvāsa Paṇḍita, Mukunda Datta, Govinda, Kāśī Miśra, and others were present there. They saw Mahāprabhu go into the temple, but when they did not see Him come out, they became anxious. They asked the *pūjāri* of the Guṇḍicā temple to open the temple doors, but the *pūjāri* answered: "Mahāprabhu has disappeared inside the Guṇḍicā temple. I saw him enter into Jagannātha with my own eyes, so I can tell you this with all certainty" (*Caitanya-maṅgala*). Other people say that Mahāprabhu left His body in the presence of His close friend Gadādhara Paṇḍita, in a state of divine possession, and that His holy remains were buried there on the grounds of the Ṭoṭa Gopīnātha temple.

The accounts of Chaitanya Mahāprabhu's life are wondrous indeed, though difficult to fully grasp. The Vedic literatures speak of great saints like Dhruva and avatars like Rāmacandra ascending into the spiritual world in the very same body. What then is the reason for doubting that Mahāprabhu could have entered either Jagannātha's body or that of Ṭoṭa Gopīnātha? Chaitanya Mahāprabhu's life is full of many miraculous events and those who find pleasure in hearing about Him will be rewarded with spiritual gifts beyond compare.

Śikṣāṣṭaka:
Mahāprabhu's Eight Summary Teachings

Mahāprabhu left behind only eight written verses in Sanskrit. These verses take the devotee from the first stage of purification of consciousness and ultimately up to the level of divine love in separation.

(1)

ceto-darpaṇa-mārjanaṁ bhava-mahā-dāvāgni-nirvāpaṇaṁ
śreyaḥ-kairava-candrikā-vitaraṇaṁ vidyā-vadhū-jīvanam
ānandāmbudhi-vardhanaṁ prati-padaṁ pūrṇāmṛtāsvādanaṁ
sarvātma-snapanaṁ paraṁ vijayate śrī-kṛṣṇa-saṅkīrtanam

"All glories to the chanting of the names of Kṛṣṇa. This chanting of the holy names purifies the mirror-like consciousness, extinguishes the forest fire of material existence, distributes the auspicious rays of the moon, is the life of pure knowledge, is the enhancer of the ocean of bliss, is the personification of the relishing of complete nectar, and cools all the souls."

(2)
nāmnām akāri bahudhā nija-sarva-śaktis
tatrārpitā niyamitaḥ smaraṇe na kālaḥ
etādṛśī tava kṛpā bhagavan mamāpi
durdaivam īdṛśam ihājani nānurāgaḥ

"O Supreme Lord! Your name bestows all auspiciousness upon the living entities. Therefore, You have expanded Your names such as Kṛṣṇa, Govinda, and so on. You have given all Your potency in those names and You have not prescribed any rules or regulations regarding when the names can be remembered. Master! You have made Your name easily accessible to the living entities through Your mercy. Despite that, due to my misfortune, I do not have any attachment towards Your names which are so easily accessible."

(3)
tṛṇād api su-nīcena
taror iva sahiṣṇunā
amāninā māna-dena
kīrtanīyaḥ sadā hariḥ

"One who considers himself insignificant like a blade of grass, who is tolerant like a tree, who is bereft of pride, and who gives respect to everyone is always qualified to chant the names of Hari."

(4)
na dhanaṁ na janaṁ na sundarīṁ
kavitāṁ vā jagad-īśa kāmaye
mama janmani janmanīśvare
bhavatād bhaktir ahaitukī tvayi

"O Lord of the universe! I do not desire wealth, followers, beautiful women, or poetry. I only desire that I can have causeless devotion for You birth after birth."

(5)
ayi nanda-tanuja kiṅkaraṁ
patitaṁ māṁ viṣame bhavāmbudhau
kṛpayā tava pāda-paṅkaja-
sthita-dhūlī-sadṛśaṁ vicintaya

"O son of Nanda Maharāja! Despite being Your eternal servant, due to the results of my own actions I have fallen into this horrible ocean of material existence. Having mercy on me, please consider me as a speck of dust at Your lotus feet."

(6)
nayanaṁ galad-aśru-dhārayā
vadanaṁ gadgada-ruddhayā girā
pulakair nicitaṁ vapuḥ kadā
tava nāma-grahaṇe bhaviṣyati

"O Kṛṣṇa! Upon chanting Your names, when will my cheeks be anointed with flowing tears, when will my voice choke up while trying to speak words, and when will the hairs on my body stand on end?"

(7)
yugāyitaṁ nimeṣeṇa
cakṣuṣā prāvṛṣāyitam
śūnyāyitaṁ jagat sarvaṁ
govinda-viraheṇa me

"O Govinda! Without my seeing You, it feels as if the time it takes to blink an eye is as long as thousands of years (*yuga*). Tears are falling from my eyes like pouring rain. It feels as if the whole world is empty."

(8)

āśliṣya vā pāda-ratāṁ pinaṣṭu mām
adarśanān marma-hatāṁ karotu vā
yathā tathā vā vidadhātu lampaṭo
mat-prāṇa-nāthas tu sa eva nāparaḥ

"Regardless of if the characterless Kṛṣṇa embraces this maidservant who is attached to His lotus feet or smashes her under His feet or breaks her heart, He is none other than the Lord of my very life air."

Many people know that Lord Chaitanya is a great, saintly personality. But, according to various scriptures, Lord Chaitanya is Kṛṣṇa Himself with the mood and complexion of Śrīmatī Rādhārāṇī. Kṛṣṇa wanted to know the greatness of Rādhārāṇī's love for Him, to relish that love, and He was greedy to know the happiness She gets from loving Him. For these three reasons, Kṛṣṇa personally left Goloka Vṛndāvana and appeared from the womb of Mother Śacī. The secondary reason for Kṛṣṇa's appearance in the world as Lord Chaitanya was to deliver the fallen souls through the congregational chanting of the holy names: *Hare Kṛṣṇa Hare Kṛṣṇa Kṛṣṇa Kṛṣṇa Hare Hare Hare Rama Hare Rama Rama Rama Hare Hare.*

Chaitanya Mahāprabhu came here to conquer people through love instead of through violence. Even great saints of the nineteenth and twentieth centuries, such as Rama Krishna Paramahamsa, Anandamayi Ma, and others, have accepted that Lord Chaitanya is Kṛṣṇa Himself. Although the scriptures describe that Mahāprabhu is the Supreme Lord Kṛṣṇa, the followers of various religious missions nowadays do not seem to accept the godliness of Mahāprabhu. Locana dāsa Ṭhākura, one of the great Vaiṣṇava poets, has mentioned that this particular Kali-yuga is the best one because Lord Chaitanya has appeared here.

Śrīla Prabhupāda Bhaktisiddhānta Sarasvatī Gosvāmī Ṭhākura reestablished the message of Lord Chaitanya through the Gauḍīya missionary movement in the twentieth century. Śrīla Prabhupada has written in his *Gauḍīya Bhāṣya* commentary that Lord Chaitanya does not come in every single Kali-yuga but appears only once in a day of Brahmā. Brahmā's one day is fourteen *manvantaras*. A *manvantara* is made up of seventy-one *catura-*

yugas. A *catura-yuga* consists of the four ages, namely Satya, Tretā, Dvāpara, and Kali (golden, silver, copper, and iron ages, respectively). In the Dvāpara-yuga of the twenty-eighth *catura-yuga* of the seventh *manvantara* in Brahmā's day,. Svayam Bhagavān Lord Kṛṣṇa, the source of all incarnations, appears. As soon as Kṛṣṇa went back to His own abode, Kali-yuga appeared. In that Kali-yuga, Kṛṣṇa appeared in the form of Lord Chaitanya to deliver all fallen souls. He came to distribute His love without discrimination in terms of caste, creed, gender, economic status, and so on.

Lord Chaitanya's main teaching is to take shelter of the Hare Kṛṣṇa *mahā-mantra*, which will cleanse the mind, heart, and consciousness, and remove all unwanted material desires (*anarthas*). These unwanted material desires are pulling us in different forms in the miserable mundane cycle of birth and death. Lord Chaitanya taught us a practice which will deliver us from this cycle of birth and death and allow us to go back to the eternal abode. As we know from *Śrīmad Bhagavad-gītā*:

api cet su-durācāro
bhajate mām ananya-bhāk
sādhur eva sa mantavyaḥ
samyag vyavasito hi saḥ

kṣipraṁ bhavati dharmātmā
śaśvac-chāntiṁ nigacchati
kaunteya pratijānīhi
na me bhaktaḥ praṇaśyati

māṁ hi pārtha vyapāśritya
ye 'pi syuḥ pāpa-yonayaḥ
striyo vaiśyās tathā śūdrās
te 'pi yānti parāṁ gatim

(*Bhagavad-gītā* 9.30-32)

"Even if an extremely sinful person renounces all worship entailed in the performance of material work and knowledge and engages in worship of Me, one-pointedly, then that person should be considered a true seeker of the Absolute Truth (*sādhu*). This is because such a person has determined the ultimate goal. Such a person will very soon become anointed with spiritual qualities and attain eternal peace. O Kaunteya! You can publicly announce that My devotee never perishes. O Pārtha! Those born in outcaste families, born as women, born in the mercantile class and born in the working class can attain the supreme destination by properly taking shelter of Me."

ā-brahma-bhuvanāl lokāḥ
punar āvartino 'rjuna
mām upetya tu kaunteya
punar janma na vidyate

(*Bhagavad-gītā* 8.16)

"O Arjuna! All souls living in the planet starting from that of Lord Brahmā down to the lower material planets are bound to take birth again. However, O Kaunteya, when one reaches Me, he does not have to take birth again in this material world."

The Supreme Lord Kṛṣṇa knew that people in Kali-yuga would be hypocritical, ignorant, deceitful, unintelligent, inactive, easily disturbed, and so on. These tendencies cause people to engage in negative actions, which do not allow them to remember the Supreme Lord and thus become delivered. Therefore, the Supreme Lord Kṛṣṇa appeared in the form of Lord Chaitanya and cleansed the dirt of the hearts of the living entities by teaching them to chant the Hare Kṛṣṇa *mahā-mantra* while being free from offenses. In this way, Lord Chaitanya showed us the path on how to go to Goloka Vṛndāvana and never come back to this miserable, material, mundane world.

Mahāmuni Veda Vyāsa is the incarnation of the energy of Kṛṣṇa who divided the Vedas and composed the *Śrīmad-Bhāgavatam*, various *Puranās*, more than one hundred *Upaniṣads*, and various other scriptures. Everything he has written is considered authentic scripture. Lord Chaitanya Himself accepts them as authenticated scriptures. We know from the *Bṛhan-nāradīya-purāṇa*, written by Mahāmuni Vedavyāsa, that in the Kali-yuga people will be delivered through chanting the holy names:

harer nāma harer nāma
harer nāmaiva kevalam
kalau nāsty eva nāsty eva
nāsty eva gatir anyathā

> "The name of Hari, the name of Hari, the name of Hari is the only way to deliverance in Kali-yuga. There is no other way, no other way, no other way."

Chanting the names of Hari is the only way to achieve the ultimate goal of human life: becoming eternally blissful. In conclusion, I would like to say again that Lord Chaitanya is Kṛṣṇa Himself. Kṛṣṇa is the Universal God. Lord Chaitanya taught us the universal spiritual practice through chanting the Hare Kṛṣṇa *mahā-mantra*. If anyone chants the Hare Kṛṣṇa *mahā-mantra* under the shelter of the pure devotees of Lord Chaitanya's lineage, then I believe that that person will be delivered from this miserable mundane world. After taking birth in eight million different types of species, the Lord gave us this rare human form. Rather than only having animalistic instinct without choice, the Lord gave humans free will; this is the greatest faculty through which one can apply the intelligence to attain the supreme destination by practicing the spirituality that was personally taught by Him in the form of Chaitanya Mahāprabhu.

I am sure that whoever, from the bottom of their heart, believes and practices the teachings of Lord Chaitanya sincerely will be delivered from the material world and attain the divine, eternal, peaceful, and blissful abode of Goloka Vṛndāvana, where the Divine Couple, Śrī Śrī Rādhā Kṛṣṇa, are manifesting eternally blissful pastimes.

MANDALA
An Imprint of MandalaEarth
PO Box 3088
San Rafael, CA 94912
www.MandalaEarth.com
info@mandala.org

Find us on Facebook: www.facebook.com/MandalaEarth
Follow us on Twitter: @MandalaEarth

ISBN: 979-8-88762-030-5

Published by Mandala Publishing for Bhaktisiddhanta Vani Publishing.

Readers interested in the subject matter should visit the Gopinath Gaudiya Math website at www.gopinathgaudiyamath.com or write to:

Ishodyan, Sri Mayapur
District Nadia, West Bengal
India, 741313

Sri Gopinath Gaudiya Math (Old Dauji temple)
Gopeswar Road, Vrindavan, Mathura (U.P)
India, 281121

Manufactured in India
10 9 8 7 6 5 4 3 2 1

ROOTS of PEACE REPLANTED PAPER

Insight Editions, in association with Roots of Peace, will plant two trees for each tree used in the manufacturing of this book. Roots of Peace is an internationally renowned humanitarian organization dedicated to eradicating land mines worldwide and converting war-torn lands into productive farms and wildlife habitats. Roots of Peace will plant two million fruit and nut trees in Afghanistan and provide farmers there with the skills and support necessary for sustainable land use.